The Trouble With Grandpa
Practitioner In Alternative Methods

Fred C. Gee

Copyright © 2011 Fred C. Gee.

Published by Fred C. Gee.

All rights reserved.

All characters in this publication are fictitious and any resemblance to real persons, living or dead, is purely coincidental.

ISBN 978-1-4709-5643-1

Illustrations by Gill Baguley.

"To all families who have witnessed and endured the eccentricities of a grandparent."

Contents

CHAPTER 1 7
CHAPTER 2 17
CHAPTER 3 29
CHAPTER 4 37
CHAPTER 5 51
CHAPTER 6 59
CHAPTER 7 73
CHAPTER 8 85
CHAPTER 9 99
CHAPTER 10 113
CHAPTER 11 123
CHAPTER 12 131
CHAPTER 13 139
CHAPTER 14 147
CHAPTER 15 159
CHAPTER 16 169
CHAPTER 17 177
CHAPTER 18 187
CHAPTER 19 201

CHAPTER 1

Vicky was late for her wedding.

The village church was full and the congregation was getting impatient.

So, too, was the handsome fellow waiting for her in the front pew. Local residents who met him with Vicky in the village had already seen why she was attracted to him.

When the bride and her father eventually arrived at the church the reason for their delay became apparent. Vicky was not wearing the dress she had meant to wear. That had not been delivered in time by a Mail Order firm and she was wearing the dress her mother wore on her wedding day. Fortunately fashions had gone full circle and the style of her mother's gown was regarded by her admirers as entirely suitable for the occasion.

The vicar performed his duties and Miss Vicky Woodfellow became Mrs Chuck Carter.

Chuck's parents had not arrived from America when the service began. The flight on which they were booked to cross the Atlantic had been cancelled and for much of the journey they were in fear of missing the wedding altogether. To Chuck's relief he met them walking up the aisle as he and Vicky moved down in the opposite direction.

Outside the church the Carters and Woodfellows met for the first time and discovered they had both been victims of industrial disputes: by postal workers in England and Air Traffic Controllers in America. Without yet appreciating the significance of that coincidence they moved into the Village Hall for the traditional Wedding Breakfast. Seeing what was spread before them the Carters said it looked more like a Sunday lunch than their idea of an English breakfast. Chuck overheard them and said they would have toasts later; and when that moment arrived Carlos, the Best Man, called on Vicky's father to give her away.

Arthur Woodfellow cast a meaningful glance at his wife and said "I don't get many opportunities to speak but I wouldn't want to miss this one. It's not that I'm glad to give Vicky away but I like to think she's giving us a son-in-law."

Vicky was heard to say she had no intention of giving him to anyone.

When Arthur sat down, Chuck's father stood up. "I'm glad it's the bride's father who gives his daughter away because after all I've heard about my son's adventures at university there'd be hell to pay if I had to give *him* away at a time like this!"

"You'll have to forgive my father," said Chuck; "he gets carried away! In fact, in case you don't know, both he and my mother got carried a long way away in order to get here. If you think they are looking uncomfortable it's because they had their passages blocked many times on their way over." This delighted his student friends who detected a *double entendre*, but Vicky's mother was not amused. She thought her father-in-law might have been an embarrassment but did not expect it to be her son-in-law who would bring colour to her cheeks. "I'm referring, of course," said Chuck, "to their various diversions when they were unable to fly from America and had to bus into Canada."

Sensing it was time to bring proceedings to a close, Vicky thanked her parents-in-law for coming over to the wedding and said she was sorry they had such a difficult journey. "I can't help thinking that if my grandfather had been there to help you, you might have had less of a nightmare. He's made a habit these days of sorting out other people's problems."

To start their honeymoon the bride and groom were duly despatched to the airport in a pony-trap, their cases littered with unhelpful labels, and their luggage polluted with rice and confetti. Coloured balloons were tied to the pony, and draped from a pole attached to the trap was a pair of knickers inscribed with the words THEY'RE OFF.

Back in the Village Hall, Vicky's grandfather, Bertrand, was chatting with a guest called Mortimer Howard who was the father of one of Vicky's student friends, and they were telling each other how their lives had changed since they were Vicky's age.

Bertrand said he had worked his way up to retirement in a local furniture business and was now finding it difficult to adjust from being a managing director to having nothing specific to manage or direct. Mr. Howard said he had a managerial role in a building society but was still subordinate to higher authority and believed he was facing the prospect of early retirement. "From what your granddaughter said," he added, "you have a reputation for dealing with problems. I'd be delighted if you could help me deal with mine?"

Bertrand looked carefully at this grey-haired man in a dark blue suit and observed an unmistakable expression of stress on his middle-aged face. "It depends," he said, "on what type o' trouble you're in."

Mortimer paused for a moment and then confessed that members of his staff had been complaining they were overworked and underpaid.

"Where have I heard that before?" Bertrand enquired.

"Of course, I know we are not unique. But these people are threatening to strike and, if they do, it will be the end of any hopes I might have of promotion."

Bertrand was not yet ready to respond. "I suppose they've been working out how much more money they would get if the firm's profits were shared among them instead of going back into the business? Well, that's one consideration, but how good is their arithmetic? I bet they haven't worked out how long they'd have to stay with the firm to make up the money they'd lose if they went on strike!"

"We've been through all that but they think I'm part of the management and simply trying to put them off. If you were in my place, how would you get over that obstacle?"

"I tell you what," said Bertrand, "suppose you come round to *my* place this evening."

It amused Bertrand that he lived in what was called a Granny Flat, for his much-lamented wife was no longer in it. Built on the side of the house in which his son and daughter-in-law were living, it had all the amenities for him to lead an independent life, but Arthur and Jane were close by to assist should they be needed. On this occasion he was fit enough, despite the day's indulgence, to entertain a visitor.

Mortimer Howard followed his host into the living room and accepted the offer of a chaser. Bertrand poured them both a brandy from a cut-glass decanter.

"So you want my advice on how to stop a strike, is that it?"

"In a nutshell, yes!"

"Right. Well I assume you are not in a position to increase their wages?"

"Right again!"

"But would you if you could?"

"Yes. I think they work hard and could get more money elsewhere if they shopped around."

"So, you're on their side, really, and not the management's?"

"You could say that."

"Then we'd better think of something that will endear you to the workers!"

"Without disgracing me at Head Office, I hope."

"That's a chance we may have to take. But from what you said earlier, you won't get many marks from Head Office if the staff abandon you."

"A classical no-win situation!"

They stared at each other for a while and then Bertrand walked to the window. It was a family characteristic, just as some people stand with their back to a fireplace when thinking.

"Would you say your staff were smartly dressed when they come to work? Or do you tolerate the trendy?"

"Certainly not! I mean ... well, they're not scruffy."

"Good. And I take it your employers would not approve if they were?"

"You're dead right, they wouldn't."

"Right. Well on Monday you call them all together and tell them to wear the oldest and zaniest clothes they can find, and explain it's the only way to convince the management they are really hard up and in need of more money."

Mr Howard was mortified!

Bertrand continued. "Oh yes, and you can suggest they bring in sandwiches to eat at lunch-time, and maybe come to work on a bicycle."

Mr. Howard rose and thanked Bertrand for his drink. "I think you're making fun of me. I should have known better."

Bertrand laughed. "Not *of* you, my friend, but if we can have fun at the expense of your management we might get them to help you out of your predicament."

"By moving me to another branch, I suppose."

"If your staff stand together as a team, your management will know they are loyal and won't want to risk losing them by getting rid of you. Don't you see, this would be a good way to improve your stock with the staff and strengthen your position at Head Office."

"That's not the way I see it."

"You did ask for my advice. Why don't you think about it? Talk it over with your wife and see what she thinks."

A month passed during which the Manager of the Blixford Branch of the *Bigstall and Longstop Building Society* tried vainly to improve his image, without daring to employ the tactics Bertrand suggested. Confined to an office, he rarely saw the public. Behind a screen of receptionists he spent his working life worrying about his staff on the one hand and his employers on the other, - failing to have much influence on either.

Like most of his staff, Mortimer dreaded Mondays. It was pay-day on Friday and there had been renewed unrest among the staff before they went home for the week-end. The atmosphere as they arrived was cold and the branch opened in a mood of gloom and foreboding. Part way through the morning, during a lull in business, Mortimer emerged from his office and called upon the staff to gather round. Unused to such ceremony they feared someone was about to be dismissed or, worse, the office was to be closed. Chairs were drawn up and papers put to one side but ten minutes later there were smiles and expressions of disbelief. By the time Mortimer returned to his office he was an undisputed hero.

Vicky and Chuck returned from their honeymoon, and moved into a small flat in a London suburb, not far from Blixford. Chuck started work as a reporter on the *Daily Pictorial* and Vicky waited to embark on a course of training in Personnel Management. At the week-end they retired to the family home in Trimstead to show off their snapshots and sunburn. The quiet village of Trimstead, in a remote part of Norfolk, is too small to appear on maps or road signs, but had probably seen better days when the county was more industrious.

After supper on Saturday evening Bertrand asked Chuck if he had heard of the *Bigstall and Longstop Building Society*. Thinking he was about to be lectured on the virtue of prudence and the need to save for a rainy day, Chuck said he was already insured and would not have enough money to invest until he proved his worth professionally. Bertrand smiled and said that could be sooner than he imagined. He then suggested how Chuck might be able to pick up a good story for his editor.

Blixford, like many suburbs, is inhabited by commuters and retired tradesmen of mixed but compatible social status. The tempo of life is moderately upbeat; dress is more casual than formal; most residents are comfortably but not particularly well off and health is a more common topic of conversation than wealth. Those who invest in a Building Society outnumber those who own shares on the Stock Exchange.

It was Tuesday morning and raining, but instead of there being a damp and miserable start to such a day, staff were arriving at the *Bigstall and Longstop* excited and cheerful. Moreover, they were all arriving much earlier than usual. Pamela, a pretty counter clerk, whose simple dress style and youthful complexion was much admired by colleagues and customers alike, had transformed her appearance to that of a threadbare gypsy and was almost unrecognised as she entered the building. Lilian, the receptionist, had abandoned the neat costume and high-rise hairstyle she usually wore and was dressed in slacks, sweater and head-scarf. John, the cashier, had exchanged a smart suit and necktie for jeans, an open-necked shirt and trainers. Tracie, the Manager's secretary, renowned for dark colours and pinned-up hair, looked quite different in a yellow blouse, blue miniskirt and over-the-shoulder tresses. Mortimer, whose concession to the charade was limited to a dark blue blazer over a clean white sports shirt and grey flannel trousers, surveyed the scene with evident distaste. He opened the doors to the public with the utmost apprehension but was secretly impressed by the extent to which his reluctant proposition had been adopted. He was also acutely aware that the staff were finding it rather fun.

By the time customers arrived cardboard boxes had replaced the once elegant waste-paper baskets and a coffee-making machine had been installed on the counter. A rack full of sales literature had been emptied and filled with bicycle chains, trouser clips and wet "sou'westers". The first customer, who was not a regular, showed no surprise and the next two or three, who had been to the branch before, stared briefly at what they saw but made no comment. One who usually stayed for a chat thought she had come to the wrong branch and left without saying a word.

As lunch-time approached the staff began to take out packages of cheese and buttered rolls, cucumbers and tomatoes, oranges and bananas.

There was a bright flash and a young man in jeans and a leather jacket stood inside the doorway taking photographs.

"Say folks, is this a party," he grinned, "or have I come at the wrong moment?"

CHAPTER 2

The staff of the *Bigstall and Longstop Building Society* were not accustomed to having photographs taken of their workplace for the management was distrustful of unsolicited publicity. They were brought up in an age when personal finance was a very private affair and discretion was more important than display. The appearance of Chuck on a day when they were quietly protesting against their employer was nothing less than a shivering embarrassment.

Pamela was the first to unfreeze. She had often imagined herself as a model and rehearsed before the bedroom mirror so the opportunity to pose for a photographer was irresistible. Forgetting for a moment that her gypsy attire was out of keeping with her dreamland image, she posed and perceived in her mind's eye a picture of herself on the front page of a glossy magazine. The thought was evidently transferred to John for he confided to Chuck that with a little persuasion he might get her to pose topless like she does on holiday. Pamela giggled and Chuck got a glorious photograph of white teeth, red lips and blushing pink cheeks.

Chuck now had the opening he needed to secure a story and he directed his first question at Lilian. "Say, just what goes on here: is this your Founders Day or does someone have a birthday? It seems like I've come to a Friendly Society, not a Building Society!"

Lilian looked awkward and appealed to John to answer for her.

"We were a Friendly Society once," he said, "but I'm not sure that things are quite so friendly now, if you see what I mean."

Chuck did not see what he meant.

"Well, the truth is," said John, "we're having a bit of a go at our management. There's a lot of competition these days with the Banks and other Building Societies all out to improve their profits, and there's not much left for us when it comes to salary reviews. Thanks to inflation, every month our salaries buy less, so we're usually broke before the next pay packet arrives."

"That's why you see us in our casual dress. 'Cos we can't afford to replace our working clothes." Pamela grinned at Chuck and he wondered what she regarded as working dress.

Tracie feared Pamela might say too much and moved to intercept her. "We are doing everything possible to *save* money," she said, "like using recycled paper, and that sort of thing, which could help a bit towards our salaries."

Chuck was not convinced. "Why don't you strike? I thought that was the usual way to express a grievance in this country."

"If we did that," said John, "we'd be worse off financially than ever. Even if it got us an increase it would take years to recover from increased pay what we would lose while striking. So, we're making our protest in a civilised manner."

"You mean, in an economical manner?" Chuck was getting the message. "Why don't more of your countrymen work that out before they take to the picket-line?"

"It's not quite the same if you belong to a Trade Union. There you have a shop steward and if he says 'out' you all go out."

"Can't *he* do arithmetic?"

"Perhaps it's just a matter of scale. If the workforce is large enough and the workers' output is valuable enough, they may get the employer to pay up before any benefit is overtaken by the cost of lost wages. If a dispute gets beyond the 'break-even' point nobody is better off."

Chuck was impressed by John's rhetoric but not by his argument. "Won't the employer be calculating the loss of productivity, and won't that put men's jobs at risk?"

"Of course, and that's another reason for making our protest this way. We think striking for higher wages is counter-productive and out-of-date."

Lilian and Pamela had been listening to this debate with open mouths - trying to get a word in. They were beaten to it by Tracie.

"Don't you think this gentleman ought to meet our Manager? I'm sure Mr. Howard would like to talk to you. ... By the way, what is your name?"

"Call me Chuck - it's short for Charlie in your language."

"You must be American, then," said Pamela, switching her thoughts from modelling and newspapers to filming and Hollywood.

Again John read her thoughts and asked Chuck if he was a tout or a tourist.

"What's a tout?" asked Lilian.

"Never mind about that," said Tracie, "I want to know the gentleman's other name so I can introduce him."

"Carter, ma'am. Chuck Carter... from the *Daily Pictorial*."

Tracie cast him a reproving look and set off in search of her boss. When they returned Pamela was having her photograph taken beside the coffee machine with a large ham roll in one hand and a can of coke in the other.

"Mr. Howard, this is Mr. Carter. He works for the *Daily Pictorial*."

Mortimer's reaction was a mixture of panic and contempt.

"Really? Have you come to report us, or will it be *distort* us?"

Chuck was ready for him.

"That depends on you, I suppose, Mr. Howard. On whether you represent the workers or the management."

"Mr. Whatever-your-name-is, in this branch we are all workers."

"Good, then you have nothing to fear from Chuck Carter. One day I may find myself in your position."

"What position is that, Mr. Carter?"

"Short of a dollar to buy a new jacket, perhaps?"

Mortimer looked down at his blazer and blushed.

Chuck took another photograph and bowed out of the building.

The story that Chuck presented to his editor was one of admiration for the enthusiasm of the staff and the liberal-mindedness of their Manager. In his report Chuck said that the staff worked through their lunch-hour, and were so sensitive to conservation and environmental issues that they used nothing but re-cycled produce. He described the atmosphere in the branch office as cordial and relaxed, befitting a business with origins in the Friendly Societies of the nineteenth century. Concluding that the art of good service was not dead, he ended by regretting that the Society's management did not appear to reward such enterprise with salaries that would enable their staff to dress in a more suitable fashion.

Chuck's editor read the draft several times and asked Chuck if he had a relative or close friend working there. "No," said Chuck, "but I've a darned good mind to put some money there - if I ever earn enough to invest any." His editor dodged the implication of that remark and despatched Chuck to a new assignment.

As soon as Chuck left the room the editor telephoned the General Manager of the *Bigstall and Longstop Building Society* and congratulated him upon a fine piece of commercial propaganda. The General Manager took this to be a sarcastic allusion to the Society's policy of not advertising in the local press, and tried to explain that his members preferred to conduct their business in an atmosphere of privacy.

"We're giving it front page treatment in tomorrow's edition," said the editor, and rang off.

Next morning a copy of the paper was placed on the General Manager's desk before he arrived at the office. His staff were buzzing with excitement and the post room clerk was running a sweepstake on how long it would be before the Blixford Branch Manager was called upon to answer for it.

Mortimer Howard spent a sleepless night anticipating the consequences of his demonstration and he was not at all surprised to be summoned to Head Office to explain. Unfortunately, by the morning none of the speeches he had practised to himself during the night sounded adequate or apposite as he prepared to meet his superior Manager.

"Did you arrange this?" asked the General Manager, pointing to the front-page photograph. "Do you allow your staff to picnic in the foyer?"

"Normally no, sir."

"What do you mean *normally*: do you mean you did on this occasion? I thought you knew it was company policy not to sink to such levels."

"I took what I thought would be the less of two evils. It was either that or a ... well, yes, that or a strike."

The General Manager did not approve Mortimer's strategy and warned him that unless he could bring his staff under control immediately he would find himself posted to another branch by the end of the week.

On his way back to Blixford, Mortimer cursed the advice Bertrand had given him - yet he reminded himself he was on the verge of losing his staff if he had done nothing. Now he looked like losing his job, and as far as he could see the staff would still be no better off. He told Bertrand it was a no-win situation!

The staff were waiting for him with good news when he got back to the branch in the middle of the afternoon. They had been inundated with enquiries and were doing better business than for many months. Practically every customer coming in had carried a copy of the *Daily Pictorial* and Pamela had already had two offers of part-time employment as a photographic model, which she was actively considering. Mortimer abandoned the melancholy into which he had drifted and sensed the opportunity to appeal against his sentence.

His opportunity came the very next morning when he received a telephone call from Head Office querying the 'returns' made by his cashier of the previous day's business. They suspected there might have been an error and suggested the typist could have slipped in an extra digit by mistake. "We are not unfamiliar with fingering errors," said the Chief Accountant sarcastically. "Surely you mean four thousand two hundred and five pounds taken, not fourteen thousand?"

Mortimer was delighted. "No, indeed, we do not mean four thousand; we mean exactly what it says. Fourteen thousand, and more to follow - thanks to the *Daily Pictorial* and a casual passer-by with a camera."

There was no call from Head Office on the following morning, although the figures before them for the second time were typical of an average week rather than a single day. When this unforeseen trend continued into a third day the company auditor was despatched poste-haste to the Blixford branch to investigate the circumstances. The auditor was accustomed to visiting branches where there was a suspicion that cash might have been stolen but this was the first time he had ever been sent to explain a surplus.

He appeared at the branch shortly before lunch, without the usual courtesy of saying he was coming. Lilian was inclined to disbelieve him when he said he had come from Head Office to see the Manager. She pressed a button under her desk to alert the cashier and command attention from the rest of the staff. The auditor ignored her suggestion that he should take a seat and hotly rejected the offer of a cup of coffee and a biscuit.

"I want to see Mr. Howard in his office, not out here like a prospective customer," he protested.

"Oh, Mr. Howard always sees his customers in his office," Lilian spluttered, "but you didn't say you were a customer, did you?"

The auditor was about to explode when Mortimer appeared, still wearing grey flannel trousers and a dark blue blazer. Neither of them had met the other before and each demanded verification of the other's credentials. That over, they moved behind the counter and headed for the cashier. John was removing a tomato sandwich from his brief-case when he saw them coming and hurriedly closed the lid before they reached him.

Force of habit led the auditor to ask John to show him what was in the brief-case. John grinned and asked if he was obliged to comply.

Mortimer decided it was time to introduce them to each other.

John then opened his brief-case and took delight in exhibiting what he called 'the elements of a poor man's picnic.' The auditor looked distrustfully at a number of brown paper bags and put his hand into one of them. Dipping deeply into the contents, he recoiled. The smell of a hard-boiled egg offended his nostrils and the soft touch of squashed tomato on his fingers repulsed him. He turned to Mortimer.

"Do you allow your staff to bring food into the workplace?"

"I think we all work better after we have had something to eat. Didn't Napoleon have something to say about that?"

John took courage from his manager and confronted the auditor with commendable candour. "We don't have a canteen out here, you know, like you people have at Head Office. On the wages we get we can't afford to eat in a restaurant."

"So where *do* you eat the contents of that repellent ... suitcase?"

"Out there, among the customers. They love it. Some even bring their own sandwiches and join us. Many of them lead lonely lives and say this is the nicest place to be at lunch-time. We never had so many people in the branch before Mr. Howard introduced this touch of informality."

Mortimer was about to demur when the auditor smiled and said "So this is why you have been taking so much money: you've turned the place into a cafe! And that's why you are all dressed as though you were on holiday."

They laughed and the atmosphere became less oppressive. The auditor explained his mission and confessed an automatic distrust of any sudden change. "When I heard you had been 'upping your take' by a factor of five I thought perhaps you were laundering some ill-gotten money from a local criminal. ... Mm, yes! ... I suppose I ought to have a look at your lunch-time customers."

Not sure whether to take him seriously, but anxious to keep him in good humour, Mortimer lead the auditor back to the reception area where Lilian and Pamela were handing coffee in plastic cups to a group of elderly customers.

The auditor studied the scene carefully, as he would have studied a set of accounts, and the smile faded from his face. "You must either sell a lot of coffee or charge a prodigious amount per cup to make the kind of turnover I've been sent to investigate!"

The penny dropped and Mortimer hastened to assure the auditor that there was no charge for the coffee. "Our increase in business is due simply to a greater awareness of the services we have to offer, and that is due largely to the publicity aroused by our local newspaper. ... Oh dear! Now that we have started to attract more custom I do hope you are not going to tell us to send them away."

"I suppose the 'services you have to offer' would not involve these attractive ladies of yours in any kind of ...?"

"Certainly not!"

"Then where is the extra money coming from?"

"Three or four of the other Building Societies, I shouldn't wonder. We are the first to break with tradition and that seems to be a plus-point, don't you agree?"

The auditor returned to his Head Office with a strange feeling that he might have missed something important, for he could not believe he really got to the bottom of the story. No-one had said anything about striking for more money, yet the G.M. had told him it was the reason given by the manager for the interest shown by the press. Well, if that was the case, why not instruct all their branches to go on strike! Surely he must have got it wrong somewhere?

The General Manager was staring at a new set of figures when the auditor reported to him in the morning. He beckoned the auditor to sit down and passed him the figures.

"Well, how do you explain those?…….. I presume you found out what's going on at the branch? Has a local bank been robbed, or are they dealing in Monopoly money?"

The auditor told of finding the staff in casual dress, serving coffee to the customers, and offered the suggestion that the manager there was carrying on a trade in other commodities in order to boost his performance and gain favour at Head Office.

The G.M. twisted in his chair and suddenly leapt up. "Dammit, I'll go there myself ... in disguise ... as a customer! What shall I offer them? Matches, or second-hand cars?" It was clear from the look on his face that he meant business.

Mortimer was in the reception area taking delivery of a stack of *Daily Pictorials* when a bearded stranger entered, wearing plus-fours and carrying a set of golf clubs. He watched Mortimer place the newspapers on surrounding tables and listened as he gave instructions to the receptionist to make sure that each of their customers took one. He held out a hand to receive his copy and engaged Mortimer in conversation. "I've heard that the Building Societies are diversifying, but I didn't know they'd gone in for selling newspapers!"

Mortimer assured him the paper was free and explained that he made an arrangement with the editor after the paper carried a story about the branch.

"Do you mean the editor pays you to give his paper away? It sounds incredible!"

Mortimer studied his visitor carefully, wondering how much he had come to deposit. "No," he said, "the transaction is purely gratuitous. He supplies the papers and we distribute them. In that way we both get publicity and our customers get something for nothing."

"I understand they also get free cups of coffee."

"Yes, that's right. It's all part of the service." Mortimer began to ask himself if that was all the man had come for. "We hope, of course, that we can help in other ways. Like investments and mortgages, for example." His tone was less friendly and he asked to be excused while he attended to other business.

The gentleman in plus-fours rested his golfing gear against a chair and sat down to read the *Daily Pictorial*. In it he found a leading article commending the *Bigstall and Longstop Building Society* for democratising its Blixford office and suggesting the practice might be extended to other places where the public are kept at bay by glass panels and closed-in counters, like banks and post offices. He slipped a copy of the paper into his bag between the golf clubs and looked around at the unfamiliar lay-out of easy chairs and low tables. His gaze turned to the brightly coloured T-shirt worn by a young woman of ample statistic who stood beside the cashier on the other side of the counter. It had a message which said BIGS ARE BEST emblazoned across the chest. From the grin on a customer's face there was no doubt that the ambiguity of the wording had been fully appreciated.

Other customers came and went, and one of them settled into a chair alongside the golfer. "Do you mind if I join you for a moment? They'll come round with some coffee if we wait awhile."

"You've been here before, I suppose?"

"Only once. I moved my account from the *Crosswich* when I heard about this place. They seem more go-ahead and with-it here and I thought I'd like to support their enterprise. As the word gets around they're bound to grow bigger."

CHAPTER 3

Mortimer Howard was called again to Head Office to meet the General Manager and was convinced he would be given his marching orders. Overnight he agonised about the likely destination of a posting, and by morning wondered if instead he might be made redundant. The colour of the door leading to the G.M.'s office seemed darker than it did the last time he was there and reflected the gloom into which his spirit had sunk.

"Come in, Mr. Howard."

The boom in the voice surprised him, but not as much as the face that confronted him from behind the desk. It was not the face of the man who a few days earlier had threatened to send him to the company's branch in Siberia. He knew he had seen the face somewhere before, yet he could not place it. There could, he supposed, be a new General Manager, but surely there would have been an announcement...

"Sit down, Mr. Howard. You're looking uncomfortable. Is there anything wrong? My face, perhaps? Maybe you'd prefer me without the mask?"

Removing first a beard and then a wig, the General Manager revealed himself as Mortimer knew him - and as the man in plus-fours who had gone to the Blixford branch to tempt him into a business deal for the sale of second-hand golf clubs.

"There are people here who were convinced you were boosting your 'Returns' by selling other commodities, not in the best interest of the firm. While I was there I saw and heard for myself what you have been doing and I must congratulate you. It took some digesting at first, and I would never have accepted the recipe if you had put it to me in words, but the proof of a pudding is in the eating and your results are proof enough for me. I propose to suggest to the Board that we copy your example, in principle if not exactly, but we will adopt a more relaxed and youthful image in all our branches. I shall consult you as we go along and adjust your salary accordingly."

Mortimer did not wait for him to continue. "That is very good of you, sir, but what about the rest of the staff?"

"I was coming to that. Of course they must also be rewarded. What would they prefer, do you think: a lump sum, or a percentage on turnover?"

"Percentage sounds rather like commission. I think they might feel it a bit old-fashioned; rather like offering them a tip. I'd suggest an increase in their salaries ... with regular reviews to allow for inflation."

"You strike a hard bargain, Mr. Howard. Maybe there will be a place for you on the Board one day!"

There were celebrations in the Branch when Mortimer got back to Blixford, but not until the customers had gone and the doors were closed did he allow a bottle of champagne to be opened. Then there was a toast to a man called Bertrand whose identity was known only to the manager.

Back in the village of Trimstead, many miles from Blixford, Vicky and her husband were spending their week-end with the Woodfellows. Vicky had taken with her a friend from the Training Course on which she had embarked to learn the skills of personnel management. Unlike Vicky, who was a complete novice straight from university, Barbara had been working for some years with a chain of retailers who were paying for her instruction and holding a job open for her when she qualified.

Chuck found Barbara more serious than Vicky and was unsure how to deal with her. He preferred the company of 'Grandfather Bertrand' who called him 'the Kid from Baltimore' and treated him as one of the family. This was something which Arthur and Jane Woodfellow had yet to do. The more they got to know him the better they liked him, but he was still only a son-in-law, and in their house a visitor on the same footing as Barbara.

It was a fine afternoon and warm and they were taking afternoon tea on the lawn, enjoying a view over fields to the river below. A motor cruiser was negotiating a mooring space and making as much noise as traffic on the road.

"Look at them tourists! You'd think by what they're wearing they'd come all the way from Africa. But they don't know how to handle boats."

"The trouble with Grandpa is he still thinks the river belongs to fishes," said Vicky, apologetically. "Like it did when he was our age!"

"When I were your age ……"

He was interrupted by an even louder noise, this time from the road leading to their house. It stopped as a van drew up at the gate. A special-delivery man got out and carried to the door what looked like a large picnic basket. Arthur rose from the comfort of his canopied garden chair and signed the deliveryman's book. He then returned with a huge hamper bearing the label: HARRODS.

"It says it's for Harold. Who's Harold?"

Jane took it from him and they watched while she pulled out a Dundee cake, a tin of shortbread biscuits, a case of

Brazilian coffee, a can of Ukrainian caviar, a box of Turkish Delights and a magnum of champagne.

"Well, who are they for," asked Arthur again, "and what has anyone done to deserve all this?" He looked from Barbara to Chuck and then to Vicky and Jane for a clue, but no-one admitted to any knowledge of the consignment.

"Why don't you look," said Vicky, "to see if there's a card inside?"

Her mother's expression suggested she had been about to do just that. Thrusting her hand into the wickerwork she withdrew an envelope on which was written the one word: BERTRAND.

There was a gasp from everyone and Jane chuckled as she passed the hamper to her father. "From another of your old lady-friends, I suppose?"

Bertrand opened the envelope and read the message to himself. The rest of the company complained and he handed the note to Chuck. "You read it, lad. You had a hand in the story, so you ought to share the message."

Pausing to study the note, Chuck had the feeling he had been an innocent accomplice to Bertrand's adventure. He then read the message aloud:

TO MY MUCH MALIGNED FRIEND FOR ADVICE THAT I WAS SLOW TO TAKE. WITH THANKS FROM ALL OF US AT *THE BLIXFORD BRANCH OF THE BIGSTALL AND LONGSTOP BUILDING SOCIETY*

An explanation was clearly called for and Bertrand recalled the approach made to him on Vicky's wedding day. "The father of that university friend of yours told me his staff were thinking of going on strike because they weren't being paid enough. All I did was tell him to get them to show how hard up they were by wearing their oldest clothes and going to work on bicycles. Seems like it got through to their employers!"

Chuck took up the story. "No, that was not all you did. You persuaded me to take my camera to a place I had never heard of, to photograph something I knew nothing about, and to make a story out of it for the newspaper. Sure, I did just that and got a picture on the front page. But it was those guys who got the wage rise, not me! I'm still waiting for mine."

Bertrand enjoyed the irony and offered Chuck a biscuit from the hamper. Chuck took one and chewed it meaningfully. "I guess you're right! That sure takes the biscuit!"

Barbara has listened to their story with admiration and moved her chair to sit beside Bertrand. She placed her hand on his knee and startled him.

"You evidently have a reputation for dealing with disputes," she told him. "Would you like to tackle another one?"

Bertrand was flattered, but cautious. He saw before him an attractive young lady whose eyes gleamed with intelligence and sincerity, yet he feared, like Chuck, that she might lack a sense of humour. That, to Bertrand, was more important than brains or beauty and particularly relevant to the question she had raised. His theory was that most crises could be defused by the injection of a little fun. The problem was usually to think of something that would reduce the tensions and lead to laughter. It meant knowing enough about the issues involved to see a funny side where others had failed. Invariably one needed an accomplice. He doubted if Barbara would fulfil that role, but was willing to play along in case he was wrong.

"You'd better tell me what the trouble is a-fore I answer your question."

Vicky's instinct was to stop her grandfather from getting involved in Barbara's affairs, but she could see that the rest of her family were agog to know more. They turned their chairs to face Bertrand and Barbara began her story........

"While I have been training with Vicky my friends in the shop where I used to work have been threatening to strike because the manager there has sacked a member of staff - for no apparent reason."

Vicky's father could not allow such a statement to pass unquestioned.

"In my experience nobody gets fired without a reason. There must be some explanation."

Barbara defended herself. "I did say 'for no *apparent* reason'. Maybe the girl misbehaved or did something the manager did not want to be copied by others. On the other hand, the manager himself might have misbehaved and wants to be rid of the girl who could betray him. The point is he did not go through the right procedures and my friends think she was dismissed unfairly."

Bertrand asked if she had consulted a lawyer.

"We don't know. Nobody has seen her since she was sent home, and nobody seems to know where she lives."

"Wouldn't it be better to leave well alone," said Arthur, still thinking in defence of the employer.

"It sounds to me," said Jane, "like someone ought to tell the police!"

Barbara said her reason for asking Bertrand to help was that the staff could not afford to lose wages by stopping work and yet they felt an awful injustice might have been done. None of them liked the manager and they feared he might repeat what he had done with other members of staff.

Bertrand said he would think about it and talk to Barbara again after they'd both had a good night's sleep. It was another of Bertrand's maxims that when in doubt - you don't ... at least, not until you've slept on it.

After sharing the contents of Bertrand's hamper they all slept well that night, but before retiring Chuck had taken Bertrand to one side and told him he sensed a story for his paper in the disappearance of Barbara's shop-mate. Bertrand confessed he might need Chuck's help if he did take on the assignment, and said they had better talk to Barbara together over breakfast.

Vicky was the first to get up in the morning for she had planned to set breakfast on the terrace and have it ready as a surprise for her mother and father - something she would never have thought of doing before she married. Chuck arrived to help when his wife was almost ready to call the others. He yawned and protested that if he'd known she was going to get up so early he would not have gone to bed at all.

Jane and Arthur were duly impressed when they found what was set before them, and only Bertrand appeared to be aggrieved. "I suppose, now she lives in the city she thinks all us countryfolk live out o' doors, like wild animals!"

"All right, Grandpa, you can have yours in the kitchen if you want. We had your treat last night. Now we're having ours!"

Bertrand put his arm round his grandchild and told her he was pulling her leg. "I don't mind a bit o' fresh air wi ' m' toast and marmalade, so long as I can sit next to your friend Barbara. I'll get *her* to keep me warm!"

Barbara smiled, but had no intention of taking him literally.

"I've been thinking about that problem o' yours," he told her when he was comfortably seated. "You'll need to fill us in with a few more details."

Chuck moved closer so he could hear the answers and Barbara told them it was a young woman called Samantha who they believed might have been unfairly dismissed. She had worked there as cashier for about three years; had never talked about where she lived nor where she came from; and spoke as if she had been better educated than the other girls.

"Apart from this Samantha, how many other people work at the branch, and how well do you know them?"

Barbara said there were six when she was there.

"Then there ought to be enough of them to find some shoes for me and Chuck if we go along to the shop next week."

CHAPTER 4

There were four shoe shops in Stillborough, all in the same street and all selling ninety percent the same shoes. The big difference, however, was that only one of them was where Samantha worked. Unfortunately, in the course of their questioning, neither Bertrand nor Chuck thought of asking the name of the shop they should be looking for.

Private telephone calls to trainees on the Personnel Management Course were not allowed and Chuck had to pretend he was a police officer in search of a vital piece of information before he was put through to his wife, having described her as a crucial witness. She, in turn, had to ask him to hold on while she whispered the question to Barbara. This brought the whole class to a standstill and infuriated the instructor whose topic that afternoon was Making Proper Use of Your Time.

Bertrand was the first to enter the shop once they found the right one, and he made a point of inspecting the shoes on display before sitting down in front of a footstool. The shop was almost empty and there appeared to be more assistants waiting to serve than there were customers. Two assistants approached Bertrand and he asked which of them was called Samantha. They looked quickly at each other and told him no-one by that name worked there any more. He noted the significance of the last two words, changed the subject, and proceeded to try on a selection of size-tens. Between fittings he contrived to keep up a conversation with each of the assistants, switching slyly from the casual to specific questions about the shop.

"How do you like working here?" he asked as the younger of the two placed his third choice of shoe on an outstretched left foot.

"Keeps me from starving!" was her only reply.

Bertrand tried again.

"I reckon it must be all right then: you don't look like you've ever starved."

It was an unwise remark for the young woman was acutely sensitive about her weight. "Does that mean you think I'm fat?"

"Good gracious no; you've got a splendid figure."

Bertrand was now in deeper trouble, because the woman was convinced he was chatting her up, which of course he was, but not for the reason she suspected.

"Do you want the shoe or don't you?" she demanded, hoping to cool any further interest he might have in her.

"I'll let you know when I find what I'm looking for," said Bertrand, "but we haven't got there yet."

"P'raps it's slippers you want!" came the cheeky retort.

Bertrand tried to dispel her anxiety, but actually added to it when he said "I was recommended to come here by a friend of mine who knew Samantha. She said 'Sam will see you all right' but as Samantha is not here I'm sure you won't mind helping me, will you?"

The young lady shot him a fiercely unfriendly look and gathered up the boxes at his feet. Another customer arrived and sat on the chair directly behind him.

"Say, miss, do I wait here or do I have to make an appointment?"

The voice was unmistakably Chuck's, but neither he nor Bertrand betrayed the fact that they knew each other.

"I'll be with you in a minute, sir, when I'm through with this customer."

Bertrand had the feeling she was through with him already, but he made one last attempt at reconciliation.

"Before you serve that gentleman can I ask you one more question? Do you know where I might find Samantha? I would like to meet her."

"No. You'd better ask the manager. He might know!"

Bertrand was left to be attended by the older assistant while the younger one, glad to escape from Bertrand, lost no time in going to the customer with good looks and American accent.

"Now, sir; can I help you?"

Chuck said he was looking for a strong working shoe that would fit a size nine foot and that it must be black or brown. "The English have a thing about men who wear colours on their feet," he said. His admirer looked at the footware he was wearing. It was two-tone blue and grey.

The fact that Chuck proved more difficult to please than her previous customer was not unwelcome. Nor did he give offence when he asked what her name was. "They call me Mimi," she said, without having any idea of its operatic association. Chuck resisted the temptation to burst into song, but followed up the familiarity by asking if she was a friend of Samantha.

"Samantha Who?"

"I don't know her other name, only I met her here the last time I bought a pair of shoes. She promised to meet me outside the cinema that evening but didn't show up."

Overcome with jealousy, Mimi told him Samantha had not been seen or heard of since she was fired by the manager.

"Gee, that's drastic. What happened? Did she get caught with her hand in the till?"

"You'd better ask the manager. He sacked her!"

Bertrand leaned back in his chair and said he could not help hearing what had just been said and was also interested in finding Samantha because he had a message to give her from one of her friends.

"Male or female?" asked Chuck with mischievous intent.

"That, sir, is a matter between me and Samantha!" Bertrand was also enjoying the charade. "Perhaps we ought to do as this young lady says and ask the manager."

"He won't tell you the truth," said Mimi.

"Oh, what is the truth?" asked Chuck, looking his admirer in the eye.

"Well, we don't know; only it wasn't fair. It was '*un*fair dismissal', that's what it was."

The Manager, who had been chatting and laughing with the cashier, and watching the two customers conversing with his assistants, decided it was time to break up their conversation.

"Is this young lady giving you any trouble, gentlemen? Can *I* help you?"

"We were asking your assistant if she knew what had happened to Samantha."

"Samantha no longer works here. Why do you ask: was she a friend of yours?"

"Yes. Can you tell us where we can find her?"

"No, I'm afraid not. You see, she left under a bit of a cloud, and she didn't leave a forwarding address."

"But you would have known where she lived when she was working here."

"I'm so sorry. It is company policy not to divulge the accommodation address of members of staff."

Bertrand said his feet were too hot now to try on any more shoes and that he would come back another day. Chuck said he would like to accompany this gentleman for a few words in private as they evidently had a mutual interest in the whereabouts of Samantha.

They had both observed the manager's expression, and his interest in the young cashier.

Chuck wondered if Samantha might have been removed to make way for this glamorous, and possibly more willing, lady in the low-cut blouse. As he and Bertrand reached the doors leading on to the street, Mimi rushed after them and thrust a piece of wrapping paper into Chuck's hand. "Excuse me, sir, but I think this fell out of your pocket."

Chuck guessed from the look on Mimi's face that she had probably given him a message, but he waited until he and Bertrand were out of sight of the shop before reading what was written on the screwed up paper. Then a broad grin fell across his face and he passed the note to Bertrand.

HOW ABOUT MEETING *ME* OUTSIDE THE CINEMA THIS EVENING? I'LL BE AT THE ODEON AT SIX-THIRTY. ... LUV MIMI.

"We'd better find out what's on, m'lad. If it's an X-certificate you may not be allowed to take her in!"

"She ain't no baby, man! And I bet she don't think like one!"

"Shall I tell Vicky you've been kept late at the office?"

"No, we'll tell her the truth: we're out on an assignment."

"We?"

"Sure! We're in this together ... though, come to think of it, you'd better watch from a distance!"

"That rules you out for the back row, then!"

"Who needs the back row? It'll be dark all over the place."

"Shall I lend you a torch?"

"You could buy me an ice cream!"

Bertrand laughed at their banter, but was thinking ahead. "If you're to keep that date at half past six, we'd better go somewhere we can discuss where all this is leading. I'll buy you an ice cream, if that's what you want, but I'd rather have a pint. Let's find ourselves a good pub."

They found there were more pubs in Stillborough than there were shoe shops and they made their choice without recourse to the telephone. The *Bricklayers Arms* had a more modern interior than its name suggested. Gone were the old divisions between Public, Saloon and Lounge bars. The entire ground floor was one large open space with a long bar extending the full length of the room. The floor was carpeted and the walls covered with pictures of office buildings and high rise apartment blocks. Evidently there was still a tie-up between the brewers and bricklayers. There was also a garden, and upstairs a restaurant. What seemed to be missing, when Chuck and Bertrand entered, were the customers.

Immediate service helped to quench their thirst, and they took their drinks to a corner seat where they could talk unheard by the barmaid.

It was agreed that Chuck would steer his admirer away from the cinema and bring her to the *Bricklayers Arms* where he would be able to see and talk to her better than in the dark.

Chuck was relieved at the prospect of sharing the interview but could not resist a last quip at the expense of his companion.

"I don't want to be rude, Bertie, but I did get the impression she was trying to get out from under your feet in the shop just now."

"O.K., I'll try not to put my foot in it when you bring her back."

It was ten minutes to seven when Chuck arrived with Mimi, and Bertrand was then on his third pint. He stood up to greet them but saw Chuck pull Mimi away and take her through a door marked GARDEN. He blinked and wondered if he had had too much to drink. Leaving his glass on the table, he headed quickly for the door marked TOILETS. On the other side of that door he was confronted by two more doors, but was unable to decide which one to use. Unfamiliar with the silhouettes he returned to the bar to ask which one was the Gents.

"I don't know what they're like where you come from, guvnor, but round here the men don't wear skirts..... It's the door on the right!"

A few moments later he was joined at the urinals by Chuck.

"What made you take her into the garden? I thought her name was Mimi, not Maud."

"I'm still on the preliminaries. I guessed if she saw you she'd freeze."

"Won't she do that in the garden?"

"No sign of it yet, but I'll take her some alcohol; that's an anti-freeze, isn't it?"

"It didn't take you long to get her away from the cinema."

"No trouble!   I said the night was young and we ought to tank up first."

"That's all right, but just remember her tank might not hold as much as yours!"

They chuckled and went back their separate ways.

Mimi had removed her jacket by the time Chuck returned, and his quick look at her bare shoulders and revealing blouse did not go unnoticed.

"I thought p'raps you'd like to see me in my off-duty outfit."

Chuck rejected the bait and diverted the conversation. He asked if she went to the cinema often and then if she ever went there with Samantha.

"No," said Mimi, "Samantha didn't like the flicks. She said she preferred to see plays and to go dancing. She was serious and clever, not like us."

Chuck protested. He said he was sure Mimi and the other ladies he saw in the shop were no less clever.

"Not really," said Mimi, "or we wouldn't still be working there."

"Why do you say that? I thought you were enjoying your work. It sure looked like you were while you were twisting those bits of leather round my feet!"

Mimi enjoyed the flattery but her smile faded as she recalled the reasons why she disliked her job. "You saw that horrible man, the manager, and you heard how rude he was. *Is this lady giving you any trouble?* Hah, that's a laugh! He meant trouble all the time."

"He seemed to be on friendly terms with the cashier."

"He's always like that with 'Miss Moneybags'. Scared she might fiddle a penny or two."

"Is that why he sacked Samantha, do you think?"

"Oh, we're back to her again, are we? No, she was too honest; she wouldn't have played that sort of game."

"Then perhaps he sacked her because she wouldn't help *him* to fiddle."

"Cor! I never thought about that. Yeah, you could be right."

"In which case, she would have known what he wanted her to do and he would know she knew, so ...."

Mimi dropped her glass. "Oh, my God - do you think .....?"

Chuck put out his hand to calm her and she grabbed it greedily.

"What can we do? He might be a murderer!"

Chuck reminded her it was pure supposition and there might be other reasons why Samantha had vanished. "Why don't we try looking for her?"

Mimi stiffened. "I see! It's her you're really interested in, isnt it? It's her you wanted to meet at the cinema, not me. Now you're trying to use me to find her for you."

Fearing that tears were on the way, Chuck took the escape route that Bertrand had offered. "I think I can prove you're wrong about that. Just stay there while I go and fetch someone who can vouch for me. He's not far away, and I think you'll recognise him." He left her looking bewildered, and returned a few moments later with Bertrand. Her expression was a mixture of disappointment and annoyance and she hastily put back her jacket to cover up the exposed shoulders and plunging neckline.

Sensing the coolness was due to his arrival, Bertrand decided it was time to mention that he and Chuck had been told about Samantha's dismissal by their mutual friend, Barbara. Their reason for coming to the shop, he said, was to see for themselves what was going on there.

Before she had time to react to this disclosure, Mimi was offered another drink. She asked, with evident feeling, for a Bloody Mary. When Chuck went to the bar to get it, Bertrand broke the news that Barbara was a friend of his granddaughter, Vicky, who was Chuck's wife. Barbara, he said, believed it *was* an unfair dismissal and had asked them to think of a way of protesting without resorting to a strike that would cost them their wages.

Mimi began to cry.

Chuck returned with the drinks and Mimi scoffed hers between sobs. "You *have* been using me, haven't you?"

Chuck was unaware of the bombshell Bertrand had just dropped. "Mimi," he said, "you're much too nice to upset. Let's tell you what we have in mind to help you and your friends make life a lot happier at the shop." He failed to realise the tears were being shed for him now that she knew he was married.

Bertrand was more thoughtful. "I suppose you *would* like us to help you?"

"What shall we have to do? We're not like Barbara or Samantha who can write letters and know how to spell."

Bertrand explained his proposal and as he did so the tears slowly turned to smiles and the smiles to laughter. A much

The Trouble With Grandpa

amused Mimi was won-over to his ploy. "You *will* come back to see how we're getting on, won't you?"

Chuck said he sure would and he still hoped to find a pair of shoes that would fit him without pinching. Bertrand said next time he expected Mimi to be able to show him something that would make them all laugh.

A week later Bertrand called at the shop again, and Mimi did indeed have something special to show him. The assistants were dressed in black instead of their customary yellow and blue, and there was a wreath of flowers at the foot of the cashier's desk with a huge card saying: *In memory of Samantha.* Triangular flag-like SALE notices, edged with black ribbon, were displayed around the walls, draped at half-mast on chromium-plated poles.

Bertrand peered eagerly around and walked quickly to a chair. He was offered a footrest on which the letters S A M were etched: a footrest that had brass handles down the sides and looked remarkably like a coffin. An air of cheerfulness surrounded him which was quite out of keeping with what he could see. Mimi stepped forward and greeted him with a mischievous smile. It was clear that his instructions had been scrupulously carried out.

He congratulated Mimi and asked if she had much trouble persuading the staff to cooperate. "Not really," she said, "Except for Hilda. She didn't care much for Samantha and thought it would be silly to wear black. So we got her to wear mauve instead, to show she's in half-mourning!"

"What about the manager? What was his reaction to all this?" Bertrand looked round to see if he was being watched, but there was no sign of the manager.

"He seems to be getting the message," said Mimi, "he made us put everything back when we moved things around and told us if we didn't wear the firm's colours he would take steps to get rid of us."

"What did you say to that?"

"We said, like you told us to, that he would then find even more coffins about the place, with *our* names on, like Samantha's."

"Then what did he say?"

"He said he'd find out soon enough who was behind our little tricks."

"Did you tell him?"

"Of course not! We said it was Samantha's ghost come to haunt him."

"Well said! How did he like that?"

"He didn't! He flew in a rage and pulled down a stack of boxes. 'Now put the lot back', he said, and stormed off into the store-room. We just laughed and pinned a poppy on each of the boxes."

"Where is the manager now? Has he given up?"

"We haven't seen him today yet. I expect he's gone to get help from Head Office. That's when the fun will start, when someone comes down and asks what it all means."

"Are you ready for that? Will you all stick together?"

"You bet!"

Chuck had joined Bertrand at the shop and was taking pictures of the coffin-shaped footrests when the Assistant General Manager of the company walked in with the shop manager. The sight of a customer standing on a chair with what looked like a shoe in his hands lead the Assistant General Manager to ask if there were mice in the shop. The manager rushed forward and was about to man-handle Chuck when Mimi stepped between them.

"These gentlemen are friends of Samantha, and they think she's disappeared because she knew too much!"

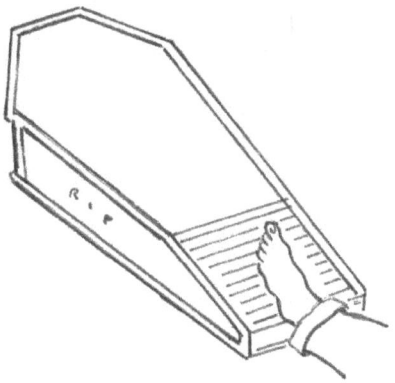

CHAPTER 5

It was a warm afternoon in late summer and Vicky had taken her husband and friend Barbara to her parents' cottage for a week-end in the country. They were having tea on the lawn beneath a large multi-coloured umbrella, in the company of wasps and dragon flies. Grandfather Bertrand was wearing a broad brimmed white canvas hat which made the umbrella redundant but the ladies were dressed to expose as much of their flesh as modesty allowed and to them the umbrella was a necessary shield from the sun, if not the wasps and dragon flies..

Bertrand and Chuck had been telling the story of their visit to Stillborough and had just reached the point at which a man from Head Office arrived at the shop where Samantha worked.

"It was the picture that did it, y'know!" said Bertrand. "I doubt if we'd ever have found Samantha if it hadn't been for that picture."

"Hold on," said Vicky impatiently, "what picture?"

Chuck glanced at Bertrand and produced from his pocket a crumpled page from a back-number of the *Daily Pictorial* on which there was a photograph of a wreath and a coffin-shaped footrest in the unmistakable setting of a suburban shoe shop. Tins and bottles of polish and creams were clearly visible with endless shelves of rectangular boxes. Notices on columns in the centre of the picture were at half-mast and the word SALE had been altered to SAM.

"So," said Vicky, "and what did that produce?"

"A man telephoned the editor to say Samantha had left home and gone abroad to another job."

"Who was it who telephoned?"

"A man with a deep voice who spoke as if he were the father."

"So she hadn't been murdered after all!"

"The editor thought it might have been the murderer trying to put him off the scent."

"That's sure how it looked for a time," said Chuck. "Then while I was in the editor's office a woman was shown in saying she was Samantha. She was surprised to hear about the phone call and said it sounded like the shop manager was anxious to kill the story because she'd never been abroad and her father had been dead for years."

"Did you tell her we thought he might have murdered *you?*"

"No, but we asked her why she thought he might have wanted to smother the story. After all, it was beginning to bring notoriety and more customers to his shop."

"Did she admit she had been dismissed?" Arthur, still wanted the employer to have the benefit of doubt, but Bertrand told him her story was she had refused to let the manager make love to her in the stock room.

"Said it was too small, I suppose!" Arthur grinned, but regretted the remark as soon as he said it. Vicky gave him a withering look and his wife slapped him across the knee with a folded napkin.

"Sorry! But why didn't she complain to the company, or tell other members of staff, - or go to a Tribunal?"

"Because he told her that if she did any of those things he would say she was a tart and had offered him sex for money."

"She could have disproved that, surely?"

"How?" asked Vicky, indignantly. "How would she prove she hadn't been, or done, such things? It would have been her word against his."

"And in those circumstances," Barbara was quick to add, "a shop manager is more likely to be believed than one of his assistants."

Bertrand sensed that Arthur was again about to defend the privileged and suggested that sometimes people invalidate what they say by the way they behave. "For example," he added, "we have reason to believe the new cashier had been taking her sandwiches at lunch-time into the stock room, followed by the manager."

"How on earth did you find that out?"

"Hilda told us. She said she had heard them giggling about it."

"Would *her* word be accepted against that of the manager?" asked Arthur.

"Two witnesses ought to outweigh one defendant"

"So, where do we go from here?"

Chuck took up the story. "You haven't heard yet what the man from Head Office had to say."

"Go on, we're listening."

"He asked me if it was my idea to turn the shop into a mausoleum. I said no it wasn't, which is true because it was Bertie's idea. But I didn't tell him that. I just said the girls were being loyal to a friend who had been dismissed without an explanation. I said they deserved all the publicity I could give them to find out why, and what had happened to her."

"That was very brave of you, darling," said Vicky. "What did he say to that?"

"He told me to get the hell out of there and said if I was a newspaperman he would sue me and my editor if we dared to publish anything about them."

Vicky looked worried. "But you did publish...or rather your editor did, didn't he? There's that picture you just showed us."

"Don't worry, honey, he can't claim damages unless his business has suffered financial loss and in fact it's been doing very well since our photograph appeared. People have been queuing up to look at the decorations!"

This time it was Chuck's father-in-law who looked worried. "Did you warn your editor about the man's threat?" he asked.

"Of course. That helped him make up his mind to print the photograph. There was nothing defamatory in that: simply news! However, once Samantha appeared he had a story and the next issue carried it in full, with an account of the erroneous telephone message and the suggestion that it might have been intended to put them off the scent."

"Wasn't that a bit libellous?"

"Someone at the shop's Head Office definitely thought so and telephoned the editor to say they had 'instructed their solicitors'. The editor was ready for them and said he welcomed the prospect of further copy and publicity for the paper. 'At the moment', he told them, 'you're getting the benefit of customer-curiosity, but when the truth is established in a Court of Law you'll find people will keep away and go elsewhere for their shoes."

"Next day," added Bertrand, who had been following Chuck's account with admiration, "we heard they had moved the manager to another branch."

"Where?" asked Barbara, her eyes agleam with relish.

"Does it matter?" said Bertrand. "We've won, haven't we?"

"What about Samantha? Does she get her job back?"

"Not at Stillborough. There wouldn't be room for two cashiers at that branch, but she's been offered reinstatement at another branch nearby. That's if she wants it. And she's been promised back-pay to when she was dismissed - on condition she gives no further interviews to the press."

"There's not much compensation in that," grumbled Barbara. "Do you think she should accept?"

"Yes," said Chuck with a grin. "The branch she's been offered carries a bigger salary and is closer to where she lives. What's more, it's where you, Barbara, are likely to be posted when you finish your course."

"How on earth did you find that out?"

Bertrand and Chuck looked hard at each other to decide who should answer.

It was Bertrand who replied. "Your friend here with the camera was asked by the shop management to drop any further interest in the matter and he made a deal with them. You'd better tell her, lad: it was your idea."

Chuck looked embarrassed. "Well, I guessed you ought to get some credit for taking up Samantha's cause. So I told them they owed it to you that there hadn't been an all out strike and it was your influence that had kept the staff together. I'm not supposed to tell you, but they said they were planning to transfer the present manager of the branch where Samantha is going to take over at Stillborough and they'd consider making you his replacement if you were willing."

"Sounds rather clever to me," said Arthur, still on the side of the management. "That way they get the best of both worlds: a bright new manager with a loyal and trusted cashier."

Barbara protested. "I think it is Mr. Woodfellow they should be thanking, not me. And Chuck, of course, but it was Mr. Woodfellow who dreamed up the tactics and saved us all a lot of trouble and lost income. If it hadn't worked out the way it has I would be leaving the firm as soon as my course is over."

"You mean you'll accept the appointment if they offer it to you?" asked Vicky who was not sure if her friend was being rewarded or exploited. "Were you expecting to be made a manager?"

"No. I thought I'd be given a desk job in Head Office, which would have bored me to tears. The prospect of going back to a shop, and being in charge of it, is quite exciting."

"Then you must bring Samantha down to spend a week-end with us some time," said Jane, who had listened to the saga with increasing respect for her father- and son-in-law.

"And I will buy my next pair of shoes in *your* shop," said Bertrand and, turning to Chuck, "which reminds me, young man, we never did finish our shopping in Stillborough, did we?"

They laughed, and resumed their afternoon tea with pate and cucumber sandwiches, buttered scones and seed cake.

Bertie and Chuck got their shoes in the end for Barbara's first act on becoming a branch manager was to send them each a pair of the best quality shoes she could find in her showroom. She also arranged for a letter to go from the company's General

Manager thanking them for their part in settling '*an unfortunate incident at the Stillborough shop.*' A scandal surrounding one branch manager did not damage the company's business for interest aroused by the newspaper story proved to be invaluable publicity. But, unlike the *Bigstall and Longstop Building Society,* they did not offer copies of the paper free to their customers.

CHAPTER 6

"I aren't a-goin' t' pretend to you, Mr. Bertie, that I'm any better off drivin' a van about fer ten hours a day an' six days a week than I were in yon factory. ..Life on the road is hard!" Bertrand was known as 'Mr. Bertie' to his employees at the furniture factory, to distinguish him from his son, 'Mr. Arthur', who took over as managing director when Bertrand retired.

Harry Chapman had been in charge of their drivers, but when he asked them to strike for more wages they did not support him and he joined a firm of hauliers where the men were more compliant. Bertrand met him again when he delivered the shoes that Barbara sent him.

"I'm sorry to hear you say that. I thought you'd found a job you liked better than the one you had when you worked for me."

"It were all right at first, guvnor but now we're working more hours for less money than when I started."

"Is it the doing-more or getting-less that matters most?"

"They both matter 'cos we don't get a choice We're just being exploited, and I don't mind telling you, Mr Bertie, I'm thinkin' o' bringin' the boys out in protest next month."

"Why next month? What's special about next month?"

"Nothing! Ev'ry month's the same where we're concerned; it's just that it may take me a month to get ev'ryone into line."

"Won't it cost you even more in wages if you go on strike?"

"Men should be prepared to sacrifice money for principle!"

"Men, maybe, but how about your wives, Harry? Don't some of them depend on their men's money to keep house?"

Harry looked shocked.

Bertrand spared him from answering. "Have you ever thought how you might get what you want without asking your mates to give up their wages?"

"Like negotiating, you mean?"

"No, I didn't mean that, because I assume you've tried that already and failed. If you haven't I suppose you think the men won't follow you. Like happened at the factory, maybe?"

"Don't remind me o' that, guvnor! But what had you in mind exactly?"

"Nothing in particular, except that it seems rather old-fashioned to stop work altogether when what you want is to improve working conditions."

"There's nothing hurts more than to cut the company's profits, and when we aren't workin' they aren't makin' profits!"

"And your men aren't earning wages. So who wins? You both go on losing until one or the other gives in. And after that it takes both sides time to recover, during which there is less to go round. All I'm saying, Harry, is that if you can find another way of making a protest you're more likely to win gratitude than scorn. Now I must go and finish my weedin'. If I withdraw my labour we shan't get any produce from the garden."

Harry stared at him ... and called him back.

"I'm sorry, guvnor, but I aren't sure what you've bin drivin' at. If there's some other way o' gettin' ourselves treated better than we are now, I'd like to know of it."

"Let me think about it, Harry. But mind you come and see me again before you take your men off the road."

Bertrand thought of little else for several days. At first he wondered why he argued with Harry at all, for he never liked him very much when he worked at the factory and he had no urge to save him from being disowned again by another bunch of workmates. Then he realised his interest was not in saving Harry but in sparing Harry's workmates from being led into a costly confrontation. He knew he would need to find out much more about these drivers and their work conditions, but he also had to be thinking of what to do if he was to help them. It seemed wrong that any of them should be obliged to work very long hours without a break, if only on grounds of public safety. But were they forced to do this or did they do it because they were greedy for more money? He began to suspect he was thinking like an employer again. But, he conceded, where greed for money was concerned, it is usually the employee who earns the profit and the employer who takes it!

The new shoes that Barbara sent him came in very useful, because Bertrand did a lot of walking while he was turning Harry's problem over in his mind. He came to think of it as Harry's problem, yet it was more his own problem, as he could not decide what ought to be done. Moreover, he was now unsure who these drivers worked for and which Union they belonged to. How silly of him to get that far involved and not know such basic facts. He sought solace in the *Pig and Whistle* and was not surprised to find Harry there already with several of his work-mates.

An hour and two pints of beer later and Bertrand had a better idea of Harry's position. He discovered that Harry and all his "mates" were working for a private Road Haulage contractor and that Harry was a self-appointed "steward" using his experience of labour disputes to rally his fellow drivers. "Resist the unreasonable hours", he had told them, "and stop work at six-thirty!" Bertrand instinctively resented Harry's readiness to stir up trouble, yet recognised the extent to which he might be justified if the examples he heard of hastily arranged long-distance journeys and frequent nights away from home were true.

His mind was made up when Charlie, one of Harry's quieter companions, whispered in his ear that if he could work fewer hours he would be content with less pay, but was afraid to suggest it.

"Why?" asked Bertrand, quietly. "That sounds a fair deal to me."

"'Cos I think they'd give me the sack if I didn't go where and when they wanted."

"Couldn't you join another company?"

"Better th' Devil you know, guv'nor! If they aren't slave drivers like ours they'd have a Union what'd take y' money one minute and lose it for you the next. One expects you to sweat, and the other to strike!"

"Wouldn't you ever strike for better conditions?" Bertrand asked, half listening to Harry urging his other mates to action.

"Not if I could help it. There aren't many other jobs in this neighbourhood what I could do, and my missus don't wan' to move."

Bertrand could sense that Harry was going to have a hard job to make his protest in the time-honoured trade union manner and resolved to help him find another way.

The interior of the *Pig and Whistle* had been modernised and, like the *Bricklayers Arms* at Stillborough, it had one long lounge with a carpet instead of sawdust on the floor; the oak beams had been fumigated against beetles, and the walls decorated with photographs instead of stuffed birds and dead fishes.

Bertrand led his listeners to a corner furthest from the door and invited them to sit with him around a table.

"I've got a lot of sympathy with you fellers if what you've been tellin' me is true - and I'm sure it is - but let me ask you bluntly, man to man, are you prepared to stick together until your employer gives way? That's if it can be done without a strike or any loss of pay?"

Harry's friends, and Harry, were confused, for it sounded to them as if Bertrand was trying to persuade them to carry on and wait until a miracle occurred.

"We aren't a-goin' t' wait fer a blue moon, if that's what y' mean!"

"No, that is not what I mean," said Bertrand, "but you ought to know by now that you can't get somethin' fer nothin'."

"You can if you're the boss, though, can't you!"

"No! Never! There's always a day o' reckonin'. And I've been doin' some reckoning for you, if you're interested."

By the way they grinned and leaned forward across the table Bertrand knew he had won their attention.

Grins turned to laughter when Bertrand told them to take their pyjamas with them next time they were sent on a long journey and to put them on as soon as it got late in the evening. The effect will be even more conspicuous, he told them, if they added an old-style sleeping cap with a bobble on it.

Harry was slow on the up-take and asked if Bertrand was suggesting they went to sleep in their vehicles.

"No, Harry," said Bertrand, winning more support as the idea registered, "I mean you to drive along as if you were about to go to bed, or had just got out of one!"

"Ah!" said one of them, "but I don't suppose Harry wears pyjamas!"

"But I bet he's got a good tassel!" said another, and the ribaldry continued while Bertrand prepared for his next instruction.

"So long as you all play the same game and stick to it, it's bound to draw attention, and I'll arrange for some pictures to be taken so that it gets into the papers."

"Hey, hold on!" said Charlie. "If my missus sees a picture of me in the cabin in pyjamas she'll get the wrong idea altogether!"

"Then you'd better make sure you tell her what you're going to do before you set out. Unless, of course, you've got other ideas as well!"

The atmosphere was now extremely relaxed and they began to enjoy the prospect of what they saw as a bit of exhibitionism. When he was reasonably sure that his plan would be adopted, Bertrand warned them that it was unlikely they would get their shorter schedules immediately, but he promised to suggest further actions until they did. Although pressed to say what those "further actions" would be, he declined on the grounds that surprise must be part of their strategy.

Chuck Carter's editor was unenthusiastic about the photographs he had been shown.

"What am I supposed to make of these? Fancy dress on wheels! Where's the story in that? Every town has its carnival at this time of year."

"These boys aren't in it for fun. They're protesting at long hours and lack of rest between journeys."

"Then what the hell are they doing in pyjamas?"

"That's it, don't you see? They're expressing their frustration."

"Well, I don't get it - and neither do you! Now, take these away and get me something interesting! And don't start wearing your pyjamas round here just because you've had something rejected."

Reaction at the Road Haulage depot was equally indifferent when vehicles were driven in by men in pyjamas. As one of the supervisors remarked, there were so many styles in men's clothing these days you never knew what to expect next. The breakthrough came, however, when one of the drivers was involved in an accident and taken into custody for "*driving while asleep at the wheel.*" The prosecution case was that the driver was evidently sleeping because he was found to be wearing pyjamas when rescued from his cab.

Chuck's editor now saw the making of a story. Under the headline: CRASH WAKES DRIVER AT THE WHEEL he printed three of Chuck's photographs to illustrate the argument that these long distance drivers were "finding their work tiresome". The owner of the Road Haulage firm involved was quoted as saying that his drivers were never short of sleep and that if some of them found it more comfortable to drive in pyjamas he had no intention of stopping them.

Fortunately for the driver concerned, a witness to the accident remembered seeing him flashing his headlights and trying to avoid a collision with an oncoming car before his van went off the road and overturned. The case was therefore dismissed and the *Daily Pictorial* carried the news under the headline NIGHTMARE FOR DRIVER IN PYJAMAS.

Round One to Bertrand!

The owner of the Road Haulage company, Mr. George Wheeler, was a no-nonsense northerner who had worked his way up from a small one-man business with a truck and a trailer to directing a fleet of heavy vehicles moving anything from shoe boxes to ship's propellers. The publicity aroused by what he called "the costume drama" performed by some of his drivers led to increased interest in his firm and to a number of new customers. Instead of threatening his men with dismissal, as some had feared, they were encouraged to continue and offered a free laundry service to keep their pyjamas clean. Harry's attempt to negotiate more wages was met with the sarcastic suggestion that by sleeping on the job they were actually saving money and ought to be paid less.

When Bertrand heard that, he was critical of Harry's haste and told him he ought to have played a different card. "I thought it was shorter hours you wanted most not more pay? You should have said you had come to talk about a 'reduction' and let him think for a moment you meant in wages. He might then have been relieved when you said you meant 'a reduction in hours' and been glad to agree!"

"Pigs might fly!" grunted Harry in response.

"But they do, my friend, they do, frequently. Dead and alive. All they need is a pilot."

Harry was not assuaged. His expectations following 'the Pyjama Game' had been thwarted and he turned angrily to Bertrand. "We did what you said, guvnor, and now look where it's got us! We're expected to go on wearing bloody nightshirts and he'll want the firm's name on them next!"

"What a good idea!" said Bertrand, "I hadn't thought of that."

Harry was about to stalk off, but Bertrand called him back.

"Hold on. There are other forms of persuasion. We haven't finished with him yet. Unless you want to give in?"

"Persuasion's no good! You'll never win Wheeler over by persuasion. Hit him where it hurts - in the purse!"

"The purse from which he pays you? That's the same as shooting yourself in the foot. Listen, Harry - we've done him a good turn, as it happens, although I didn't plan it that way. Now, if we play our cards right we could get him to be a little more cooperative when it comes to working out your journey schedules."

Harry listened to Bertrand and went back to his mates with a new idea.

The following evening, Mr. Wheeler was in his front room, at home, watching television, when the sound from his receiver was obliterated by noise from a passing lorry. It began with intermittent blasts from an oncoming hooter and swelled to a crescendo as the vehicle drew level with the house, then faded as the driver moved on. There was a short pause in which he tried to recapture the missing part of the programme he was watching, until the sequence of noises-off was repeated. The second vehicle appeared to be even larger or more heavily laden, for besides the angry growl of its hooter, there was a rumble of tyres on the road, making the floor of the house vibrate. After another pause, a third and then a fourth truck went by with similar disturbing effects. Mr. Wheeler was shaken into thinking the army was on manoeuvres and went to the front door to investigate. He was just in time to recognise the registration number on the tail end of a lorry as it lumbered by with its hooter wailing. It was the first time he had known one of his own trucks to be routed past his house which nestled in a quiet stretch of countryside more than a mile from the motorway.

Next morning Mr. Wheeler called the Depot Manager into his office and demanded to know why so many of his company's vehicles went past his house the previous evening, and why they were making such a hideous noise. The Depot Manager looked surprised and protested he had no idea that any had gone in that direction, since all the trucks he despatched had actually passed *his* house 'by mistake'.

Mr. Wheeler and his Depot Manager were not the only executives of the Haulage company to have been disturbed by passing traffic for a thorough investigation during the morning revealed the full extent to which Bertrand's ploy had been adopted. One by one the drivers were interrogated and each in turn told of congestion and fatigue, leading to frustration and impatience. None of them admitted to conspiracy and all expressed surprise that they had wandered into 'executive territory'.

Mr. Wheeler was convinced there had been a coordinated resistance, but determined to ignore it. "We must ride out the mutiny" he told his senior staff, "and they must continue to ride out their schedules!"

Bertrand was pleased with the solidarity of his disciples but sad to find they were making such little impression on their employer. Perhaps his victories over the shoe shop manager and the Building Society had been too easy. Or was it that corporate bodies were quicker to respond to criticism than one-man employers? He pondered the problem and decided to persuade Harry to vary the tactic.

Next evening, as soon as it got dark, the vans, trucks and lorries belonging to the haulage company sounded their horns continuously as they drove through the centres of neighbouring towns and villages. To Bertrand and Harry's dismay, no more notice was taken of them than the regular sirens of racing police cars, rescuing ambulances and flat-out fire engines. The public was so accustomed to those percussive sounds that they took them in their stride and strolled on regardless.

In contrast to Bertrand's reaction the men were beginning to enjoy their protests and paradoxically looked forward to their late night schedules. Without further encouragement they repeated their tuneful processions through the high-streets and contrived to return whenever possible via the homes of their executives, especially in the early hours of the morning. So long as the goods and consignments got through to their customers, George Wheeler was unmoved, even by the grumbling of his executives whose wives were angry at their loss of sleep.

A month passed and the enjoyment began to wear off. Harry and several of his drivers were mouthing their unrest in the *Pig and Whistle* while Bertrand listened thoughtfully. Suddenly their attention was diverted to the screen of a television set mounted on a shelf above the bar. They saw a line of lorries drawn up across a road at the exit to a dock. The road signs were in French but there was a queue of trucks with British number plates waiting to drive out.

Harry was ready to sympathise with the British drivers but Bertrand teased him by asking if he thought they ought to cross the picket line.

"Bloody French farmers, I reckon! We oughta do the same to them and their damned apples."

"Maybe we ought to do the same to Mr. Wheeler." The idea was Charlie's and was greeted with general approval ... until Bertrand asked whether he meant to stop Mr. Wheeler's lorries getting out or Mr. Wheeler getting in.

"I ha'n't thought o' that," admitted Charlie, "but I don't reckon it'd matter which!"

Two days later, when the word had been passed around, all of Mr. Wheeler's vehicles took to the road with a resolute driver determined to teach an obstinate employer a lesson in logistics. Each driver had been carefully briefed to return via Mr. Wheeler's residence and to park his vehicle in the road near to Mr. Wheeler's house. It was dark by the time the first one reached the rendezvous and no-one saw the driver step down from his cab and place by the vehicle a notice stating the time at which it was left.

At intervals throughout the evening other vans and lorries arrived and their drivers departed, each to be picked up and driven to their homes by an elderly gentleman in tweed suit and deerstalker hat.

At first light the following morning, the road was blocked by a solid mass of vehicles all bearing the Wheeler name and each one displaying a card with the time at which it was parked. Mr. Wheeler was awakened by a policeman at the front door of his house and asked if he had been holding a party or intended to use the road as a regular parking area for his company's transport.

Standing on the doorstep in his brightly coloured dressing gown Mr. Wheeler surveyed the scene and was photographed alongside the policeman by a press man with a camera. The photographer then walked along the line of stationary vans and lorries, adding to his collection of pictures intended for the next edition of the *Daily Pictorial*. Mr. Wheeler attempted to restrain the press man by grabbing at his leather jacket and reaching for the camera, but was held back by the policeman and advised to calm down with a cup of coffee and whatever else he had for breakfast. Red in the face, he went inside and slammed the door behind him. The policeman pulled out his portable radio and asked for the vehicles to be towed away before the morning rush hour if they had not by then been collected by their owner.

The Trouble With Grandpa

The Depot Manager was roused from his bed by a furious employer, and in turn set about telephoning all the drivers he detailed the day before, demanding to know where they left their vehicles overnight and insisting they collect them immediately ... 'wherever they are.'

One by one the drivers reported to the depot, clocked in, and set off on foot or bicycle to collect the van or lorry they abandoned. Some, whose next consignments were urgently required, were rushed to the scene in the Manager's car. Each one was met by an enraged Mr. Wheeler who stormed about the pavement outside his house shouting abuse and ordering them to get their vehicle back to the depot faster than he could reach it by telephone! One or two drivers were duly intimidated and sped off regardless of the speed limit; others deliberately stalled or flooded their carburettors to delay their get-away.

That afternoon, while Mr. Wheeler dictated letters of warning to each of his drivers, preparatory to terminating their employment, the editor of the *Daily Pictorial* studied the pictures which Chuck took and congratulated him on a worthwhile story. The editor then commissioned an article on the anti-social attitude of the haulage contractor who disregarded the safety of the public by making his drivers work excessive hours at the wheel.

Unknown to Mr. Wheeler, his Depot Manager contrived to withhold delivery of the warning notices, hoping to persuade him not to alienate his men any further. Next morning, when the *Daily Pictorial* appeared with a selection of photographs and a highly critical editorial, copies were taken to Mr. Wheeler's office by every member of his staff and the atmosphere of an impending storm engulfed the depot.

Mr. Wheeler arrived with a copy of the paper under his arm and immediately called for his Manager.

"Did you send out those letters?" he demanded.

"Well no, not yet, but they're all ready to go. I'll see to it right away."

"Oh no you won't! Thank goodness I can rely on you to take your time! I've got a much better idea. Get this letter I've just written typed up and send it round to the *Daily Pictorial* before they put the next edition to press."

"Do you want me to read it first?"

"Dammit man, you will whether I say yes or no, so get on with it!"

The letter acknowledged the editor's concern and said that in return for the loyalty his drivers had shown by not taking strike action to support their grievance they would be given new schedules to limit the hours they were asked to work.

"Now you know what it says, you'd better draw up some new schedules."

CHAPTER 7

Chuck's photo-journalism earned him enough credit with his editor to be assigned to one of the paper's leading correspondents as his Assistant. "Pop" Andrews was a big man, physically and professionally. He had red hair and a reputation for independent thinking. Chuck described the one as bloody and the other as cussed, and frequently ran both epithets together.

It soon transpired that Pop's reason for wanting an Assistant was not to fulfil a desire to teach or inspire a promising apprentice but to provide himself with an understudy when calls from his editor to cover newsworthy events coincided with something of greater personal interest. Chuck accepted the subordinate role with equanimity, but increasingly resented the attribution of an article to his superior when it had been written by his assistant, especially when the superior had been nowhere near the event he was claiming to have witnessed.

Chuck confided his resentment to Bertrand, and the temptation to take seriously the old man's advice 'to invent an event' was overwhelming.

A week or two later the *Daily Pictorial* carried a story that Government Offices in the heart of London were the scene of a mysterious fire and that confidential papers had been washed into the drains of Whitehall after thirteen fire engines failed to put out the blaze. 'The fire is said to have started,' said the report, 'in the belly of a newly-appointed Minister who was more *in a state* than *of it.* The fire then spread through the internal ventilation shafts, carried on hot air from the

Conference Room. Firemen were prevented from reaching the source of the fire for several minutes by having to sign in at the security desk. A messenger on the third floor suffered a broken leg by falling over a length of red tape which he failed to see against the background of flames.'

The report went on to say that papers with the tell-tale words Government Property were later seen floating on the lake in St.James' Park and have been fished from the River Thames by anglers on the banks of the Tower of London. A photograph of the recently appointed Secretary of State for Education pointing to a Bunsen burner and surrounded by schoolboys in a chemistry laboratory appeared in the same column.

The story did not lead to a libel action, nor to the dismissal of its author, but was widely acclaimed as the best of the year's send-ups on April the First. Unfortunately for Chuck, he had attributed it to Pop who took all the kudos.

Meanwhile, Vicky completed her training in Personnel Management and was practising her skills with an Employment Agency, engaging and deploying recruits for the highly lucrative market of Office Temps.

One day a young woman of her own age came to be interviewed and was recognised immediately as a contemporary at Redbrick University. Penny had studied History against Vicky's Modern Languages, but she had failed to find anyone who would pay her for the knowledge she had gained. She was quick to tell Vicky she had also failed to find a man who would keep her, so in order to earn her own living she had been obliged to learn shorthand. Vicky studied her carefully and decided not to point out that some people earned their own living as well as having a man-about-the-house.

"Can you type?"

"If I have to."

"Can you make tea, answer the telephone, and deal with amorous advances?"

"Do I have to?"

"What kind of work is it you are looking for?"

"What would I have to do to get your job?"

"Six months on a Training Course!"

Later that day Penny found herself 'temping' for the Senior Partner of *Spanners and Boult*, a firm of Consulting Engineers. Theodore Boult, 'Teddy' to his partners, was having to deal with pressure from his staff to reduce their working hours at a time when business was far from buoyant. He was unsure if that was because fewer people were in need of consultation or more consultants were offering their services but he was due to retire shortly and needed every hour that could be charged to clients if he was to recover the capital he invested in the firm. Hours meant money to consultants.

Paradoxically, he resented having to pay an Agency an hourly rate for the services of a secretary, especially as he knew he would be unable to keep her fully employed a hundred per cent of the time she was there.

"I suppose you can use a typewriter?" His opening gambit took Penny by surprise. She smiled and waggled her fingers at him. "That's like me asking you if you can count."

Teddy was duly contrite.

"Forgive me, but I've had so many applicants who say they only work with a word processor, and we still use an old golf-ball."

"I was brought up on golf balls: my father had a dreadful handicap!"

The Senior Partner decided it was time to get down to work.

At lunch time Penny returned to the Employment Agency and invited herself to lunch with Vicky. They settled down in a Pizza Parlour and spent a convivial forty minutes reminding one another of days on campus, chuckling at mutually amusing anecdotes and frowning at moments they would have preferred to forget.

"You must come to our flat one evening and meet my husband."

"Would that be safe, do you think?"

"I don't know, but he's never run away before!"

Grinning broadly, they each paid their bills and returned to their respective employers.

Chuck was curious to meet Penny after hearing of Vicky's encounter. "She sounds cute! Will she take over from the old man when he retires, or will he take her with him?"

Vicky smiled. "I would rather have her as a friend than an employee."

"Guess that goes for us too, eh?"

"Sure!" said Vicky, mocking his accent.

Supper at the Carter's flat was usually a casual process of passing various items of food through a burst of micro-waves and forking it off a plate balanced on the knee in front of a television set. On this occasion, however, Vicky had set the dining table with place-mats, cutlery and wine-glasses, and Chuck had produced a bottle of Beaujolais and a bunch of flowers. A large stew-pan on a gas ring in the kitchen emitted odours which drifted through the building and greeted their guests as they arrived. Chuck had remembered Pop Andrews' advice about the importance of presenting a balance in all things, so he had invited his best man to keep Penny company. It was Carlos who arrived first.

"Wow, you kids must be in the big time, or else getting old, to put out the dishes for poor little old me!"

"Don't kid yourself, buddie boy, this ain't just fer you. Wait till you see the 'dish' that's comin'!"

"Stop it, you two. You're in England now; let's be English, shall we? Pour yourselves a drink and make mine a martini. It'll give you both somewhere to put your hands when Penelope arrives!"

Chuck and Carlos exchanged glances and signalled each other to do as they were bid.

They were standing with arms folded when Penny entered the room. Vicky could tell from the look on their faces they had met Penelope before. Carlos was surprised but appeared delighted; Chuck was amazed and seemed embarrassed; Penny stared uncomfortably at one after the other and then turned to Vicky.

"My dear, you didn't tell me *you'd* done the rounds at Redbrick!"

Vicky was quick to catch on. "This is my husband," she said, dragging Chuck forward with one hand, "and this is our best man," grabbing Carlos with the other. "How come we never all met up at College?"

Carlos hastened to admit he knew Penny in his first year at College and said he introduced her to Chuck in a moment of careless abandon. Chuck corrected him and said he also met Penny when he first 'went up', but stood aside when she showed a preference for Carlos. They both stressed that all this happened before Vicky came onto the scene. Penny quickly confirmed this by saying they were each in her address book under the letter C but she had moved on to K by the time she left College.

Preliminary drinks, and further unlikely revelations, relaxed the atmosphere and by the time they reached the dinner table they were in excellent humour. Having temporarily exhausted the most intimate recollections concerning themselves and one another, their conversation turned to some of the other students they knew and interest was expressed in the whereabouts of everyone they could remember. Among them, the name of Virginia Howard was mentioned.

Carlos looked wistful. "I guess old 'Ginny' was what you English call a dark horse. She never had much to say, but gave you the feeling there was plenty to find out about if you bothered."

"Did you put that theory to the test at our wedding?" Vicky asked.

"No," said Carlos," I was too busy doing my official duty of keeping an eye on your husband."

"On our guests, more likely!" said Chuck.

The reference to Miss Howard provided Vicky with a cue to redirect the conversation and she told Penny how Chuck and her grandfather had helped Ginny's father escape a nasty situation at his branch of the Building Society. Penny was intrigued and asked Chuck if he made a habit of helping young lady's parents out of difficulties.

"Not only their parents," said Vicky, and went on to describe his involvement in the affair of a missing shoe-shop assistant. "Show them your photographs, darling!"

Chuck pretended to object, but then obeyed.

Penny was impressed. "Remind me never to tell you anything about myself that I don't want to appear in a newspaper!"

"Is there any such thing?" Carlos asked, and got a clip from the back of her hand.

Next morning, when Penny went in to her boss to take dictation, she found him in a reflective mood. Instead of replying to letters, or drafting reports, Mr. Boult wanted to off-load some of his anxieties.

"Some days ago you asked me if I could count. Do you remember?"

Penny blinked, and waited for the rebuke.

"If I were to ask you whether you could multiply, what would you say?"

Penny said nothing but thought she was about to get an unusual approach of a personal nature. Tilting her head, she opened her mouth and raised her eyebrows but found no words to answer.

"Thirty-seven and a half multiplied by, say, fifty ... that's half of 3,750, in case you haven't got there. In other words, 1,875. Now, suppose we multiply just 35 by fifty, what do we get? 1,750. That's less than 1,875 by 125."

Penny was already hopelessly lost, but relieved to find her initial fears fading.

"As mere numbers they may mean nothing to you, of course, but if we think of them as pounds-sterling would you not say they were important?"

Pounds-sterling were as important to Penny as pounds-avoirdupois, but she was not yet sure where the drift was leading.

"How many young men, do you think, would be prepared to spend £125 per week for the sake of half-an-hour a day?"

Oh dear, thought Penny, we may be back on the slippery path again!

"Perhaps I haven't made myself clear," said Mr. Boult in a flash of understatement. "Out there, in those offices, are young engineers who want me to cut their working week from thirty-seven and a half hours to 35, and since their average charge-out rate is £50 per hour that would reduce their potential earnings by £125 per week. Do you think they would let me cut their salaries by that amount?"

Penny was beginning to think that if he continued to expect her to solve his management problems she was already underpaid.

Mr. Boult instinctively read her thoughts. "Why am I asking you all these questions, Miss Atkinson? Because, I suppose, I need to reassure myself that I am not dreaming. There are ten young engineers out there, so it isn't even as little as £125 per week I am likely to lose: it's £1,250 ... or more than £50,000 a year!"

Penny was now overwhelmed with all the figures and felt it was time to intervene. "You could refuse, I suppose."

"I could, of course. And they could all leave and go to work elsewhere. This is a highly competitive business now, you know. As the big industrial companies cut down on their staff more of them become consultants. Firms like ours are springing up like mushrooms."

"But if they go to work for another firm in the same line of business, won't they still be on thirty-seven and a half hours a week?"

'Teddy' was taken aback. This girl was brighter than he took her for. "True," he admitted, "but the more pressure there is from young men like ours, wherever they work, the sooner it will happen that we all have to cut back to 35 hours a week. And I have just been explaining what that will do to our income."

"You could, I suppose, put up your hourly rates." Penny could see she was treading on dangerous ground.

"I've just told you, the market is much more competitive these days. We'd probably lose more business that way than we would lose staff if I don't agree to their proposals. It's a no-win situation, wouldn't you say?"

Penny made a last effort to assist. "Have you ever thought of engaging a consultant to advise you how to deal with a dilemma like that?"

Mr. Boult was thunderstruck! For years he had persuaded directors of other companies to employ his firm to handle their problems, but never before had anyone had the temerity to suggest he might seek the help of another consultant to handle his own problem. Sensing his reaction, Penny explained that she had heard of a man who recently helped solve a number of difficult cases involving staff disputes and said she could arrange for Mr. Boult to meet him discreetly if he wished. "No-one else need know", she added.

Bertrand was boiling an egg when the postman delivered the invitation. By the time he finished reading it the egg was hard. Typed on plain, unheaded notepaper, it left him none the wiser as to its author.

"Dear Mr. Woodfellow,

I wish to consult you on a matter of some delicacy. I will be grateful, therefore, if you would treat this approach with the utmost confidence.

I shall explain all when I see you, and trust you will accept this letter as an invitation to dine with me on Monday next.

It has been suggested that you will recognise my <u>bona fides</u> by the fact that I have booked a table for two at the Riverside Hotel in Trimstead for seven o'clock.

Yours truly,

Theodore.

It had been signed with a fountain pen, not a biro.

The Manager of the *Riverside*, Mr. Petro Polanski, was an American, well known to Bertrand who was no stranger to the hotel. Nevertheless, Petro was surprised to find his friend visiting so early in the morning. He asked to be assured that nothing was amiss; that 'Bertie' brought no bad news; and that he had no complaint to make against the staff!

Bertrand hastily dismissed such fears and quickly came to the point.

"Who booked me in for supper next Monday, that's what I want to know?"

Petro was taken aback by Bertrand's abruptness and protested he had no idea they were to have the pleasure of his custom on that evening. A check of the register showed that the only booking for the evening had been made in the name of a Mr. Theodore.

"Who made the booking?" Bertrand asked.

The receptionist looked thoughtful. She said she remembered taking a telephone call from a lady who said she was speaking on behalf of Mr. Theodore. "She sounded like an educated lady - from London, or Oxford, or somewhere like that. I thought by the way she spoke that you must know the gentleman."

"Didn't you ask for an address or a contact number?"

Petro and Bertrand shook their heads reproachfully.

Unable to account for the invitation to dine there on Monday evening, Bertrand returned home and spent the weekend pondering over possibilities. Several scenarios occurred to him. One grew from a fear that his success as a suppressor of strikes had become known to a foreign power who wanted to recruit him for an act of sabotage or assassination. A more romantic supposition was that he was about to meet with a plenipotentiary from Downing Street or Buckingham Palace to help resolve a political or royal dilemma away from the glare of media publicity. Yet the vision which brought him down to earth and eventually displaced all others was that he was about to have the table turned on him by a practical joker.

On Monday evening he reached the hotel half an hour ahead of the appointed time, took a brandy-and-water from the bar and looked out over the driveway where he could see everyone arriving. After some minutes he took from his pocket the invitation letter and read it again: '*I wish to consult you on a matter of some delicacy.*' Of course! Why had he not spotted it before? Matters of delicacy invariably involved acts of infidelity! He was about to be confronted by a man who had to choose between a wife and a lover, or between a lover and disgrace! What an old-fashioned drama that would be! Surely that sort of thing was commonplace nowadays? Would anyone bother to conceal it?

Bertrand's thoughts were so disturbing that he failed to see a car drive up and the driver enter the hotel. His daydream was interrupted by the Manager addressing him with untypical formality.

"Mr. Woodfellow, allow me to introduce 'Mr. Theodore'. Mr. Theodore, this is Mr. Woodfellow, a very old friend of ours."

"How do you do, Mr. Woodfellow? Does he mean you are very old, or just an old friend?" It was a clumsy attempt at a joke and left Petro dumbfounded. Bertrand, however, was delighted. He parried the joke immediately.

"Is Theodore your first name, your surname, or a nom-de-plume?"

"Touche!" said Mr. Boult, and they settled down to a welcome aperitif.

CHAPTER 8

Bertrand was surprised to find himself at ease with Mr. Boult. He had imagined he would be meeting a suave or inscrutable man in his mid-forties, immaculately dressed with a rose or carnation in his button-hole; a tall and elegant figure, clean shaven and heavily perfumed; attractive to the ladies and condescending to strangers. Instead, he found a man not far short of his own age, quietly dressed in a light grey suit, small in stature but strong of limb, white haired and charming. As they were led into the restaurant the man he mistook for a dandy suggested they dispensed with formality and asked Bertrand to call him Teddy. That, he said was how he was known to his partners and friends. Bertrand wanted to ask him by what name he was known to his staff, but thought better of it.

"All right, Teddy," he said, "and you can call me Bertie; that'll make us both feel a lot younger."

The two men faced each other across a large table arranged for them in a remote corner of the restaurant. They studied the menu and ordered their meal. Then Teddy explained why he was seeking Bertie's advice. He told of how the young men in his firm were agitating for a shorter working week, and how difficult it was for a Senior Partner to steer a course that was fair to his staff and profitable to his partners.

Bertrand listened attentively. There was something about the man that appealed to him. He spoke plainly and modestly, with an air of authority: firm and calm on the outside, yet soft and uncertain within.

When he had told his story Teddy refilled his glass and took a long drink. It was his turn then to make a visual assessment of Bertrand. While he was preparing for what he had come to say, he had observed Bertrand only as a stout but healthy-looking countryman with a rugged exterior and a colourful dialect. Now he was aware that below the surface which had long been exposed to country air there was solid character and sensitivity. Bertrand had exhibited the virtues he admired most in men: the ability to listen; to wait until spoken to before offering an opinion. Teddy liked what he now saw and reciprocated Bertrand's feeling of friendliness and trust.

"I'm told you've a reputation for dealing with problems like mine. Have I been correctly informed?"

Bertrand had already abandoned his vision of matrimonial conflict but had not had time to reflect upon the circumstances just described to him.

"I'm not sure that I welcome the image of being a man with a reputation. People are very narrow-minded down here, you know! It's true I've tried to put a bit o' common-sense into a few folk who'd got out o' their depth a bit. But I can't say as I reckon you'd be short o' that commodity."

"Flattery, my friend, is all very well, but if we're to work together as fellow consultants, we'd better be frank with one another: I'm in very deep water indeed, and I don't know how long I can stay afloat."

Bertrand liked the idea of being called a 'fellow-consultant', but he wondered if his qualifications for practising such a trade would be enough to satisfy and rescue a professional.

"I can't say as I've come up against your type o' trouble afore. I'm an old employer myself, as you probably know, but since I retired I seem to have been on the side of the workers. I had a case where some drivers in a haulage company wanted to cut down on their working hours, but they were doing twice as many hours a week as your chaps, and I reckoned they were being driven too hard. So I backed them against their management. In your case, if I understand it, a small cut in working hours would soon lead to zero profit."

"And zero working hours for everyone!"

"For everyone, or just some?"

"In my firm, everyone, because the partnership hasn't got the capital to meet the extra costs, even if we could hold our fee income at the present level. And I don't see how we could maintain that level if fewer hours were being worked."

"Surely you're not booking a hundred-per-cent of everyone's time to your clients are you?"

"No, of course not, but how do you get more out of less? If staff work fewer hours they will have less time available for doing what they have to do for a client."

"Wouldn't morale go up, and more chargeable work get done during working hours?"

"My experience tells me that any morale-boost would be short-lived and it would not be long before we were back to the old level of output."

"So! If you can't raise efficiency, how about raising your fee rates?"

"That way we would lose clients. No offence, my friend, but I've been over all these text book remedies and I've come to you as a last resort because somebody told me you have unorthodox ways of getting results."

Bertrand grinned. "Ah, I see, I'm a quack now, am I, not a consultant?"

Teddy relaxed. "Let's say you're a practitioner of alternative methods."

"All right," said Bertrand, "I've got the message. But it takes time to get results. To start with, I need a few more facts."

Teddy was quite forthcoming in responding to Bertie's questions about the size of his staff, their whereabouts and work routines, and the number and roles of other partners, but when Bertie asked him if he had a sense of humour he began to wonder if he had been the victim of a confidence trick or fallen into the hands of a joker.

Bertie hurriedly explained. "My maxim," he said, "is if you can't crack a problem by serious means, try cracking a joke! Or, put another way, if ordinary methods fail, try fun!"

Teddy now suspected the wine had gone to Bertie's head.

Observing the absence of a smile on Teddy's face, Bertie leaned across the table. "Look here, bor, I know you like a leg-pull, 'cos you pulled mine when we were introduced. What I'm saying is that laughter sometimes breaks down barriers and maybe I'll think of a way to apply that principle to your problem. The point is, of course, if I do - will you carry it out?"

Teddy's expression was one of disbelief. "Well I'll be darned! I never thought I'd pay anyone to make fun of me! How much do you charge for that? Or should I ask how many working hours you need to create a joke?"

Disbelief turned to incredulity when Bertie told his host that he made no charge at all for his services.

"It's been a pleasure meeting you," said Bertie, "and I've thoroughly enjoyed the meal. I retired from work a long time ago and I've got enough money to live on. What I do with my

The Trouble With Grandpa

time now is freely given. Reward is finding the remedy, and getting the right result."

Teddy stood up and shook Bertrand by the hand. He paid the bill with a sense of anticipation, and his journey back to London seemed shorter than when he came. Bertie stepped briskly back to his cottage and reflected on the task he had accepted. Why, he wondered, was there never anyone like himself around to dispel the problems he encountered when he was Managing Director of the furniture factory?

The new Managing Director of the furniture factory was surprised to receive a visit from his father during working hours on the following morning.

"What would you do if the staff here said they wanted to do less work for the same money?"

"I'd fall off my chair laughing!" said Arthur. "They couldn't work less than they do now if they tried!"

Without knowing it, Arthur had given his father the very idea he needed.

The telephone in Teddy's room at *Spanners and Boult* rang when Teddy was out of the room. It was answered by Penny Atkinson. In her acquired telephone voice she announced herself as 'The See-nior Partner's temp'ry sec-ret'ry' and asked who was calling. On being told, the pitch of her voice changed.

"Oh, hallo Mr. Woodfellow. I'm afraid Mr. Boult is out of the office at present. Can I get him to ring you back or would you like to leave a message?"

"Just tell him I've had an idea, will you. That should please him, don't you think?"

"Oh yes, I'm sure it will; but am I to know what the idea is?"

"Afraid not! It mightn't work if anyone knew about it."

"What, not even Mr. Boult?"

"Ah, well, but you're not Mr. Boult, are you!"

Penny was cross, and her voice resumed the higher pitch. "No, of cawse not. I quait understand! I'll give him your message. Good afternoon!" Then, as an afterthought, she added : "Give mai regards to your grand-daughter. Vicky and I were at College together y'know."

She did not wait for a response, which left Bertrand looking vacantly at the handset of his telephone.

Vicky did not often get a telephone call from her grandfather in the middle of the day and her first reaction was to suppose something had happened to her mother. "No, gal, there's nothin' t' worry about. It's just that I've discovered who t' thank for that dinner I had last night at the *Riverside*."

"It wasn't me, grandpa!"

"No, but it were a friend o'yours who works for an engineer in the City. A man called Boult. D'y'know him?"

It took Vicky a moment or two to realise he had worked out that she must have been responsible for arranging the rendezvous with Penny's boss.

"Was it a good dinner, grandpa?" she giggled. "And is he a nice man?"

"Yes to both those questions, but next time you set me up like that please give me warning, cos I might have turned up in m' fishing clothes."

Vicky explained that *Spanners and Boult* were clients of the agency she was working for and that she and Chuck had been telling her friend Penny about some of his recent ventures into industrial relations.

"Shall I tell Chuck to get his camera ready again?"

Bertrand said that wouldn't be a bad idea, but he'd rather not say anything that would get back to Penny.

Teddy returned Bertrand's call that evening from his home. "I got your message, Bertie," he said. "Better if we discuss it away from the office. Lines do get crossed occasionally, you know. Especially if there's a nosey telephonist on the switchboard."

"Sorry if I embarrassed you but I wanted your approval before I go any further. Are you prepared to spend a pound or two to persuade your boys not to push you into shorter hours?"

Teddy jumped. "I thought you said you didn't charge for your services?"

"I don't. But the plan I have in mind will involve purchasing some new equipment."

"Not a computer, I hope?"

"No, but it may cost you as much."

"How much?"

"How much will it cost you to lose two and a half hours a week from all your staff?"

"Too much! I told you, it will cripple us."

"Then it'll be worth half that much to be spared, wouldn't you say?"

Teddy was aghast. "Hey, steady on! That would be ... I'd say that would be ... five figures, wouldn't it?"

"Call it an investment," said Bertrand, "or an insurance."

"I call it extortion! What kind of equipment are you talking about?"

Bertie hesitated. "Something quite novel. Made to measure. Distinctive. Designed to support your position. For a modest outlay."

"It had better be a small one!"

"Oh, ah! I can promise you that!" said Bertie with a chuckle. "If you'll trust me in principle I'll get you an estimate and explain everything later."

"I'm not in the habit of signing open cheques, you know."

"I'm only asking if you're prepared to write one out. You won't have to sign it until you tell me to put the work in hand."

They agreed to meet again after Bertrand obtained a quotation.

Arthur received another visit from his father. Staff in the furniture factory began to speculate on the Old Man's return as M.D., but Mr. Bertie had no such intention. He walked into his old office and grinned at the new incumbent.

"Could you make up a special order of office furniture and deliver it for next Bank Holiday?"

"Hold on, Dad! That's rather a tall order, wouldn't you say?"

"I'm not sure you'll call it that, m'boy, when you see the drawings!"

It took them a week for designs to be drawn up and costed. That left six weeks before the Public Holiday. Work in the factory was relatively slack, so Arthur told his father they could start on the job as soon as he confirmed the order. Arthur was puzzled by the nature of the project but was assured there was a perfectly proper purpose to which it would be put.

Teddy was quite agreeable to another meeting at the *Riverside Hotel*, which he found enchanting on his first visit, but he was horrified at the thought of it costing him possibly thousands of pounds. When Bertie outlined his plan, however, he collapsed - not with horror but with laughter, and the two men spent a hilarious evening contemplating the outcome.

By morning, Arthur had permission to proceed.

During their next visit to Trimstead Vicky and Chuck were recruited to help deliver some goods to *Spanners and Boult* over the coming Bank Holiday week-end. Curious, but willing, they committed themselves to the task and promised to say nothing about the assignment to Penny in case she inadvertently spoiled the fun.

Rumour in the factory was that the special order was for export to Japan. This got modified to the belief that the items they were making would go to a Japanese family who were about to settle in the village. Neither story escaped beyond Trimstead, however, and the staff at *Spanners and Boult* remained unaware of what was coming to them.

On the first day of the Public Holiday week-end Chuck and Bertrand helped to move desks, chairs and cabinets from the second floor to the basement of an Edwardian Terrace in south-west London and adjusted the position of telephones, light fittings and door handles in each of the rooms while Vicky and her mother applied their knowledge of needlework to the curtains. Meanwhile, at Trimstead, Arthur prepared to load his delivery van with items designed to replace those which Chuck and Bertrand were moving to the basement.

The second day of the Holiday period was a Sunday when roads and pavement around the Terrace were empty of traffic. At 10.30 in the morning a van stopped outside the offices of *Spanners and Boult* and Arthur unloaded the new furniture.

Bank Holiday Monday was the day when people returned from long distance journeys, or slept in for an extra hour in the morning and spent the rest of the day lazily in the garden, in a pub or an easy-chair; but for Bertrand, Chuck and Theodore Boult it meant none of those things. Items delivered to Theodore's office the previous day had still to be put in place and various re-arrangements made to the lay-out in many of the rooms. By the time Teddy was satisfied, and Chuck had taken a number of photographs, it was late in the day and they were ready to move to a nearby Eating House for hearty helpings of Deep-Pan Pizzas, swilled down by carafes of Valpolicella.

Teddy normally arrived at his office before any of his Partners, but on the morning after the Bank Holiday he was there before any of his staff. His policy of open-door management was known to be more symbolic than literal and it did not surprise the other early-arrivers to find all doors in the establishment were closed. What did surprise them, however, was the unfamiliar interiors when they opened the doors to their rooms.

One by one, members of staff moved from room to room, curious at first and then incredulous. By the time the last of them arrived the others had assembled in the library to compare notes on what they had seen.

They were there chattering excitedly when Penny appeared with a message from the Senior Partner that they must all attend a meeting in the Board Room at 12 o'clock. She was catechized to explain the meaning of it all, but denied having any inside information. All she could tell them was that her typewriter now had a short carriage whereas last week it had a long one.

Desmond was the youngest member of staff, who had recently joined the firm from university with expectations of steady employment and increasing salary. He supported the idea of a shorter working week, which seemed to him 'progressive', but he was not a belligerent campaigner. The room which he shared with Hector, who was a vociferous advocate of reducing the standard week, looked larger than hitherto and had an almost doll-like quality. The desks were smaller and lower and, like the chairs, had shorter legs. Lamps hung nearer to the ceiling, and were encased in close-fitting shades. A four-drawer cabinet had been replaced by one with only two drawers, and a shelf on the wall for reference books had been shortened to accommodate a row of filing boxes.

Unnoticed at first, but discovered when he returned from the library, the telephone lead in Desmond's room had been shortened and no longer reached his desk from Hector's. A tiny flower-pot on the window-sill held a miniature rose instead of the fuschia an aunt gave him for his birthday, and behind it the curtains were hanging well above the sill instead of some way below it.

Occupants of the room next door were staring at similar alterations and offering various explanations to account for them. James, who was a wag, suggested that everything had shrunk because water had seeped through the ceilings while they were on holiday, but his room-mate, Jeremy, thought it more likely the partners had been persuaded by the female staff to set up a creche.

Further down the corridor, older members of staff had reached the same conclusion as those at the furniture factory and speculated an imminent take-over by the Japanese.

Alone in the library, the librarian noticed a shelf filled with paperbacks which she remembered had once held large dictionaries and professional year-books.

Midway through the morning a tea-lady arrived to administer refreshment to the keyed-up consultants and found her pantry filled with crockery designed for drinking Turkish coffee.. She protested she was not going to run backwards and forwards all morning refilling those stupid cups and was not pacified when someone suggested they might be easier to wash up.

Inside the Board Room a Partners' Meeting was in progress and Teddy was defending the tactics he had employed to show staff what it meant when a vital resource was shortened. One of his partners told him he ought to grow up and another said it was time he retired, which he considered cancelled each other out. He chided them for not supporting him and asked if they would rather see the firm go bankrupt.

"It's your house and mine that are at stake," he reminded them. "We are not protected like shareholders. The moment our liabilities exceed our assets we have to stop trading, or risk going to prison. It's not only the balance sheet that puts firms like ours on the rocks: it's lack of cash. Some months we don't have enough cash in the bank to pay salaries. So we borrow, but two or three bad months in a row and the lender calls in his loans. That means putting our hands in our own pockets. Do you want to risk that?"

The link between a shorter working week and a weaker cash position did not elude them and they gradually came round to recognising the need to resist what one or two of them had begun to feel was a legitimate claim.

"I'd rather fight to keep the firm in business, so everyone has a job and a wage, than give in to keep the peace and then have to fight off the liquidator."

Teddy had made his point and the meeting ended in accord, if not in harmony.

At 12.30 the Board Room was full of staff, but none of the partners. When the partners did arrive they were led in by Theodore whose appearance stunned his audience. Accustomed to seeing him in a dark suit and collar-and-tie, they were unprepared for his appearance in safari shorts and a

T-shirt. His fellow partners followed, looking flushed and embarrassed. They sat down at a table facing the staff and Teddy rose to speak.

"I daresay some of you imagine we have been making fun of you. Well, maybe now you can have some fun at my expense! They say a good laugh can break down barriers. Sometimes a joke touches a chord of understanding. So, I'd like you to join me in laughing at what you've seen this morning. It may not seem funny to you now but if it sticks in your mind it may do later. You see, when you asked me for a shorter working week I had to ask myself what that would mean to the firm. The more I thought about it the more I could see us being short of the things we needed to keep going. You could say you would work harder in the time you were here, but that would imply you aren't working as hard as you might do now. If I thought that, I would be asking you to work longer hours! No! I had to convince you what shorter hours would mean. Not shorter desks, perhaps, but fewer of them. Not shorter curtains at the windows, but it would certainly mean 'curtains' for some of you!"

It was a longer speech than he intended but delivered with such panache, and so close to lunch-time, that no-one contested or contradicted anything he had said. Staff left the room in little groups, smiling or sniggering at his "costume", and the partners gathered round him to express their relief that his strategy seemed to have succeeded. Indeed, in the pubs and coffee bars to which the staff retreated there was general agreement that 'the old man' had made out a good case and deserved to be supported.

Desmond spoke for many of them when he said: "He had a bit of courage at his age to dress up like that and confront us all with unpopular news."

Hector put the alternative viewpoint. "He certainly dressed-up the story, I'll grant you that!"

Teddy returned to his room to change and found Penny waiting admiringly at the door to congratulate him. He smiled and put his hand on her shoulder. "Please convey my thanks to that friend of yours - and, of course, to Mr. Bertie!"

CHAPTER 9

Teddy had one more card to play, and it earned him a decisive trick. Having played his joker, he presented a trump that won back support from members of his staff who had been offended or alienated by his attempt at humour.

After an extended lunch-hour, he visited each office in turn, inviting the occupants to help him replace their newly acquired items of furniture by those still stored in the basement. So relieved at not having to spend the remainder of their working days in reduced circumstances, their residual anger subsided.

Teddy's problem then was what to do with a collection of miniaturised items that were unlikely to have any second-hand resale value. His partners not only wanted some of their money back but also the return of space being occupied by unwanted specimens in the basement.

Once again Bertrand came to the rescue. He telephoned Teddy to enquire how the staff reacted to their strange surroundings and said he had a suggestion to offer for disposing of items that were now surplus to requirement.

"You're thinking of all those splendid desks and chairs we took down to the basement, I suppose," said Teddy, grudgingly.

"What! You don't mean they're still there, do you? I reckoned they'd all be back in their old positions by now and you'd have a load o' collectors' items on y' hands!"

Teddy could hardly believe it. Bertie knew the staff would not take kindly to working in a Lilliputtan environment and had discussed with Arthur the possibility of buying back the diminutive furniture to use for display and publicity purposes. Arthur had been reluctant at first to consider this, but brightened to the idea when his father suggested there might be a market for hiring it out to advertisers for use with children and chimpanzees in television commercials.

Days later, a pantechnicon arrived at the *Spanners and Boult* offices from the Trimstead factory and took away what the partners regarded as unwanted relics of a troublesome episode. The staff lined up to see them go - and bade farewell, at least for some time, to their 35-hour week.

At a desk in the offices of the *Daily Pictorial,* Chuck was saying good-bye to the prospect of having his photographs published. He accepted Bertrand's advice that if they were displayed publicly in a national newspaper it would defeat the object of his exercise, for it would not contribute to the improved relations between staff and partners at *Spanners and Boult.* He was compensated later when he learned they were to be used to advertise the products of his father-in-law's factory, but he could not disguise his disappointment when he admitted to Vicky that the trouble with her grandpa was that he had a conscience as well as a sense of humour.

Chuck had always been on good terms with Bertrand but relations with Vicky's father had not always been so close, for Arthur was unsure of Americans, suspicious of youth, and envious of those who had been to a university. Above all, he resented the fact that Chuck had now become part of the family. However, the incident at *Spanners and Boult* had helped to overcome some of the prejudices for his readiness to shed his jacket and get his fingers dirty showed him in a different light. Vicky was less surprised, for she had watched him with his sleeves rolled up fixing cupboards to walls, curtain rails to window frames, and shelves to just about everywhere. She was delighted to hear a warmer tone in her father's voice when he spoke to her husband.

"Are you enjoying your job as a journalist ... Chuck?" he had asked when they were at lunch on the Sunday after Bank Holiday. The pause before he mentioned Chuck by name indicated how difficult it was for Arthur to bring himself to say the word, but Chuck took comfort from the question. Even so, he could not yet allow himself to reply with comparable familiarity and baulked at calling him Arthur or father-in-law. He remained: Mr. Woodfellow.

The verbal relationship with his editor was similar. Staff on the *Daily Pictorial* were known by their first names, or some by their nicknames, but the editor was Mr. Reid to all of them. On the premises, that was, for there were variations by which he was known in the local pubs and eating houses. Chuck had so far taken care not to be overheard repeating a pseudonym, although he had whispered some of the more colourful ones to Vicky on occasions.

Not long after the episode at *Spanners and Boult*, Chuck was called to the editor's office and given an assignment that at one time would have gone straight to Pop Andrews.

"I want you to get yourself an interview with Nigel Slipstream. He's the local whizz-kid who runs a factory on the Industrial Estate next to an old airfield at Whetford. I hear they're making a new bi-plane capable of taking off and landing on a football pitch. Find out if it's true and what his plans are for selling it. Should make a good story. Take a camera and be sure you get a picture of it."

Chuck did some homework and found that the factory belonged to a small private company of which Mr. Slipstream and his wife were directors and principal shareholders. The business began in an old hangar which they leased from the

Air Ministry, and with staff they recruited from ex-RAF technicians living in the area.

It was something of a surprise, therefore, when Chuck arrived at the factory gates to be greeted by a uniformed security guard and confronted by an extensive complex of modern buildings. His vision of a remote workshed with a corrugated iron roof and a handful of elderly engineers in oil-soaked dungarees was quickly shattered. There were awkward moments while the guards at reception checked his credentials, which had been artfully prepared in advance by a compositor in the *Pictorial*'s print room, and there was a silent sigh of relief when he was allowed to proceed to the Managing Director's Office. This, he was told, was on the top floor of a three-storied block about half way between the gates and a tarmac runway. There was then the inevitable outer office in which the formidable M.D.'s Secretary was sitting.

"Good morning, young man. I understand you wish to see Mr. Slipstream about an order for our new aircraft?"

"That's correct," said Chuck, moving towards a door marked PRIVATE.

"The M.D. will see you shortly; he's tied up on the telephone at present. Of course, you're very lucky, he would normally expect you to see our Marketing Director first, but he's out of the country this week. Have you flown in from Baltimore this morning?"

"Kind of you to ask," said Chuck, "but no. I've been hopping around Europe, looking for what's noo. Drove up from London this mornin' to take a whiff of your Norfolk air. They say it's good for geese and turkeys, so I guess it's O.K. for flying."

Miss Plumb was not amused, but gave him a chilly smile.

The Trouble With Grandpa

When Chuck met the Managing Director he received another surprise. Nigel was not the severe-looking bald-headed war veteran he expected to see but a middle-aged man with a youthful manner and casually dressed. On the far wall behind a large desk was a huge portrait of a man in a flying suit who Chuck assumed was the founder of the firm and, by the likeness, father of the present Managing Director.

"Good morning Mr. Slipstream. Thank you for seeing me at short notice."

"At no notice at all, you mean!" Mr. Slipstream looked up from the documents that his Secretary had just given him.

"I see from your papers you are described as an American Purchasing Engineer and a member of the Baltimore Union of Microfliers."

"I'm afraid, sir, that is a little misleading. You see, I have a confession to make. That document was faked to get me past your security. I've not come to buy one of your air-planes but to write about them. My editor thinks you've got a product that would make a good story, and that you might be glad of some publicity. I can see you're a busy businessman, but I'd sure like to take that story."

Nigel Slipstream was torn between rage at the impudence of this young man who had cheated his way into a sanctum, and admiration for his audacity which he would be glad to encourage in his salesmen.

"Well, now that you're here, you might as well stay. But I'd better warn you, I don't like giving interviews. What do you want to know?"

"Is it true you're making an aircraft that will take off and land on a football pitch?"

Nigel roared with laughter. "That must be a joke put round by our Supporters Club. I don't suppose you know, but I'm Chairman of the local Football Club?"

"No, but I guess that figures. It would be appropriate, wouldn't it, for you to turn up at a match in your own flying machine: but is it true?"

"Before I answer that, where do you come from? How do I know you're not a spy from a rival firm?"

Chuck placed before him his *Daily Pictorial* staff pass and added: "I wouldn't know who your rivals were, at making planes or playing football!"

"Would you know a good aeroplane from a bad one?"

"Probably not, but I can tell from the look of this place that you don't make rubbish."

"Good. That's the right place to start. We make 'kites of quality'! That could be our slogan, only we don't go in for catch-words. We've never needed your kind of publicity because our products sell themselves. What's more, they introduce new customers. It's sometimes more difficult for us to build enough than to sell what we make."

"That sounds pretty, but how long can it last? I mean, with rising costs of raw materials, bought-in components and staff wages, won't you price yourselves out of the market, sooner or later?"

"You sound like an economist!"

"I was, as a student, but it taught me not to practise as an expert!"

"A pity they didn't teach a few more to think like that! Costs are not a problem where a commodity is in demand, as you well know. In our case there is an even bigger demand for jobs than there is for what we make. There is more unemployment around here than there are spectators at a Cup Final. So, while we are able to satisfy our customers and design for the future we'll stay in business and keep our workers."

Chuck picked up the cue. "It *is* a new idea you're working on then? I mean, it may not land on a soccer pitch, but it is something new?"

"All right, I'll tell you what it is, because it won't help you know how to make it. Our designers have produced a revolutionary model for business executives: a small lightweight two-seater that will fly off a back lawn - if the garden's big enough. But the real secret is its price and performance; its complete airworthiness and ease of handling. It's Air Miles away from any rival and we've already got a big order from the Germans. I tell you, there'll be a long waiting list as soon as the first ones are airborne."

"Jeeze, you don't mean to say, they haven't flown yet!"

"Of course they have! A prototype was certified by the Civil Aviation Authority last month. But we're not yet tooled up for production."

"Could anyone else move in on your market while you're tooling up?"

"Not unless they've seen our drawings, or stolen the prototype."

"Who might have tried to do that?"

"At one time I would have said the Russians, but nowadays I doubt if they would be interested. More likely to be the French. They've got an active aircraft industry and a long established envy of the British."

"Can you trust all your workers to keep that sort of secret?"

I trust my workforce to want to keep their jobs. That's why I don't expect any trouble about their wages."

"Which is how you are able to keep down the price!"

"Exactly. Now is there anything else you want to know, because I have an appointment with someone who gave a legitimate reason for coming to see me."

"Yes, but I don't suppose you would allow me to take a photograph of the new model?"

"You're darn'd right I wouldn't!"

On leaving, Chuck noticed a chromium-plated miniature in the shape of an aeroplane on the desk occupied by the M.D.'s secretary. It was attached to a vertical rod on a circular base, and appeared to be acting as a paper-weight. He took a snapshot of it with Miss Plumb in the background, and hurried out.

Vicky was not often able to accompany her husband on his work assignments but she had persuaded him to drive her part of the way and leave her on the edge of the industrial estate to do some shopping. As they could not be sure how long Chuck's interview would last, or indeed if he would get an interview at all, they had agreed to meet up again in the lounge of the *Pickwick Hotel*, on the road by which they came.

Chuck reached the hotel before the shops had shut and was not surprised to find that Vicky had not yet arrived. He settled into a comfortable armchair in the lounge and ordered a tray of tea and muffins. (Tea he could get at home, but muffins were a treat!) Thus refreshed, he reflected on the meeting with Nigel Slipstream and wondered what kind of a story he could write that would satisfy his editor. He tried out a few headlines, hoping a story would flow from one of them : -

"Back lawn take-offs for top executives."

"Soccer boss unafraid of strikers."

"Bosch to buy revolutionary aircraft."

"APE reporter BUMs way into aircraft factory."

He was still chuckling to himself over the last of his suggestions when Vicky appeared, carrying a large bag naming the store from which she had purchased a new coat.

"Guess that'll take the grin off my face!" said Chuck.

"Not when I tell you who I met in the shop."

"Go on, tell me : Father Christmas!"

"Not quite. Do you remember Tom Bishop, your engineering friend at Redbrick?"

"Good God! Did he get a job as a shop assistant? Don't tell me he sells lady's underwear!"

"No, but he may have been buying some. I met him with his wife while I was browsing over coat racks."

"So, he's married too, is he? I always said he'd have one screw too many!"

"Don't be so vulgar! They'll be here in a minute. I invited them to join us for a meal in the restaurant."

Although they did not know it at the time Tom Bishop was a member of the production team at the aircraft factory which Chuck had just visited. He had taken a day off from work to join his wife at a pre-natal clinic in order to get himself accepted as a spectator at the birth of their forthcoming baby. Their presence in the department store was to buy Sara a maternity dress, into which she had changed by the time they arrived at the *Pickwick*.

The exchange of pleasantries when they met would be better described as a volley of good-humoured abuse, for it was clear that Tom and Chuck had been accustomed to a robust relationship. Fortunately, Vicky and Sara had it in common to have each studied modern languages, albeit at different universities, and they left the men to work out their exuberance at the bar while they sat at a table with their drinks comparing notes and waiting for the call to go in for an early dinner.

Conversation at table came faster than the service. Much faster! By the time their orders for food had been taken they had exchanged memories of student days and brought each other up-to-date with their domestic arrangements. Between the first and second courses they related for the benefit of Chuck the circumstances of their meeting that afternoon. Tom admitted he had recognised Vicky before she identified him, which Sara said confirmed her opinion that Tom had put on weight since they married. Tom grinned and said : "hark who's talking!" Vicky followed his eyes and said when Tom introduced Sara as the mother-to-be of his child she was unsure whether or not Sara was also his wife. Chuck recounted his adventure of getting into the aircraft factory and greatly amused Tom with the details of his subterfuge. Of course, he said, if he had known Tom was working there he would not have needed such a ruse. Tom disagreed and said Nigel Slipstream would never have authorised an interview. "Then it's a good thing we didn't meet sooner because I wouldn't have wanted to tell my editor the man wouldn't see me."

"Well, since you did see him what are you going to tell your editor?"

"I'm not sure. I haven't written it up, yet. But I've thought up a few headlines and I'll work backwards from those. Take a look and tell me which one you like best."

Tom read the list and raised his eyebrows at the pun about a football chairman being unafraid of strikers.

"Did he say anything to you about a strike?"

"Only that he didn't think one likely."

"Did he say why?"

"Yes. He said there were enough unemployed in the neighbourhood to fill a football ground, or something to that effect, and no-one would want to put his job at risk."

"Well, I'm afraid he's wrong about that. There's a lot of pressure building up in the factory for a shut-down if they don't get a rise soon."

"Won't that result in the firm losing the German order for those new aircraft."

"He told you he'd got the order, did he?"

"Why, isn't it true?"

"It won't be much use to us unless we can produce the goods, and so far we've only made a couple of prototypes."

"Would the Germans go elsewhere if you failed to produce?"

"No, they'd go without. No-one else is making that sort of kite."

"Then it's not a question of having to keep the cost down?"

"He gave you that idea, did he? No, I think he could afford to charge more and then he could pay us more. He's just being cautious - or mean!"

"I'd say he was being prudent."

"And I'd say you were being naive!"

Sensing they were about to enter turbulent waters, the wives called for more wine and steered the conversation towards less serious subjects.

It was nearing midnight when they got home and Vicky made quickly for her bed. Not so, Chuck, who picked up the telephone and called Bertrand.

"Hiya, grandpa! ... Bertie, are you awake?"

"Aye, but if I weren't I would be now! Is anything the matter?"

"Yeah, I've got a problem. A real problem."

"A real problem, eh? That must be something to do with drink, or drugs, or women. Which is it?"

"It's none of those, Bertie, it's ... it's kind of ethical."

"Sounds like drugs then, though I'd have said by your voice it were drink!"

"Bertie! This is serious. I've got an article to write for my editor and I don't know if I should tell him all that I've found out this afternoon."

"Does that mean you want to tell me, instead?" Bertrand was now wide awake.

"The problem, Bertie, is that if I report what the Managing Director told me I will be giving ammunition to the work-force to 'down tools'. On the other hand if I report what one of his staff told me I will probably lose them an important order that will put them all out of work for good. What do you think I should do, Bertie?"

"Could you write about something else?"

"That would put *me* out of work! I was sent to get a story ... and I've got two!"

There was a long silence in which Chuck feared Bertrand might have hung up, and Bertrand thought Chuck must have gone to sleep.

"..... If I were you - which at the moment I'm rather glad I'm not - I'd go sick tomorrow."

"I guess I'm feeling a bit that way now!"

"Well, sleep on it, lad. In the morning it may seem clearer what you have to do. Pretend you're an engineer and you're designing a bridge or a new building. It's your job to see it won't fall down. You check everything and, when you're satisfied, you stick to your convictions. The same rules apply to a good journalist. Maybe that's why there aren't many of them! Can I go to bed now?"

"Thanks pal. Sorry I kept you. G'night."

Chuck did not sleep well. He turned over many times in his bed, and many ideas in his head. If he were to paint a glossy picture of a modern factory led by far-sighted entrepreneurs who were throbbing with enthusiasm from ground floor to Board Room, making revolutionary aircraft for wealthy executives, would that inspire the staff and bring the company more customers, or would it inflame them.? Or would it just encourage competition?

...On the other hand, suppose he slipped in the rumour of a low-paid workforce, would that persuade buyers they were getting a good deal; or would they detect the risk of industrial rebellion and be frightened off?

...What if he told a different story: that the product was so good that everybody would want it; that the Germans had booked it and the French wanted to copy it. Then he could suggest business would be so good that the workforce would earn bonuses and the local community prosper. Surely the Managing Director would get the message? Or, would he?

Perhaps he should be a politician and write about the splendid opportunity created by a new invention for employer and employees to benefit. That is if workers could help to keep down the cost, and managers could keep up morale on the shop-floor.

Or should he consider *his* employer's profit and be sensational? Reveal the threat of a walk-out when the company was just on the threshold of success? Compare the modernity of the premises and the luxury of its interior to an outdated style of management and relative poverty of its workers?

Daylight crept in, and it was time to get up and make himself a coffee. He took Vicky a cup of tea, and set about writing the article that had floated around in his brain all night.

CHAPTER 10

It was late in the morning in Trimstead and Bertrand was reading the Sports section of the Sunday newspaper when Chuck and Vicky drew up in their second-hand sports car. He put the paper to one side and asked if Chuck had brought him the latest issue of the *Daily Pictorial*.

"We couldn't forget that, grandpa," said Vicky, throwing him first a kiss and then the newspaper.

"Where's the 'Special Correspondent'?"

"He's putting the car away. Says it might rain."

"Did he take my advice?"

"Take a look for yourself." Vicky was clearly proud of her husband, and pleased to observe her grandfather's opinion of him.

What he saw in the *Daily Pictorial* was a photograph of a well-dressed secretary with hand outstretched towards a model aeroplane spiked to a paperweight beside a telephone. Below the picture was the caption: *DESKTOP AIRCRAFT FOR TOMORROW'S TYCOONS.* The accompanying article called it a revolutionary aircraft and gave a brief indication of its projected performance. It also included a pen portrait of the Managing Director of the firm that would make it, and a reference to the possibility of competition from the French if the company failed to get production out on time.

After lunch the Woodfellows settled themselves round a fire in their spacious drawing room. Arthur nodded off in his armchair, Jane studied the paper's Colour Supplement and Vicky the fashion pages. Bertrand and Chuck slipped into the study and spread the *Pictorial* between them.

"You've kept your powder dry, I see. That was very wise. Neither side can take offence at what you've written, but they both ought to be reading between the lines."

"Do you think they will? Tom said there was a move on the shop floor to join a trade union."

Bertrand posed another question. "How seriously does the man you interviewed fear his business being taken away by a rival company?"

"More than he fears his workforce taking to the picket-lines, I should say."

"Do you think he has any evidence, or reason for that fear?"

"Only that he seems to distrust the French."

"Ah! Then I think we ought to encourage the fear he has, so he never has to face the other danger."

Chuck had no idea what Bertrand was getting at but could see from his expression that he had a plan in mind.

After tea, while the others were in the television room watching a romantic drama on the screen, Bertrand said he believed he and Chuck were witnessing the prelude to a tragedy. He likened it to standing at the bottom of a hill listening to the rumblings of an advancing avalanche, or the roar of an erupting volcano. Chuck was accustomed to exaggeration, but regarded this as a little over-the-top.

"Are you thinking of the loss to mankind if we don't get a lightweight aircraft that can land on a bottle-top, or are you worried about the setback to Nigel Slipstream's profits if his men stop working?"

Bertrand said he was shocked. "Now that you know what is going on, how can you stand by and watch so many people get hurt without trying to stop it happening?"

"What do you think I should do? If you're right about a volcano or an avalanche, what chance have I got of stopping it?"

"I think we should try."

"O.K. I'll get Vicky to help me get up a petition!"

"It's not a petition we need, it's a letter to your editor."

A letter, printed in the *Daily Pictorial* a few days later, referred to its previous report of a revolutionary new aircraft and suggested that a joint venture with the French, like that on Concorde, would be good for both countries and a solution to possible staffing problems.

The retort from Nigel Slipstream in the following day's edition of the paper drew on the analogy of two cooks in the same kitchen and reassured readers that the aircraft would soon be flying over their heads for everyone to admire. Tom was asked by his workmates what he thought would have given Nigel the confidence to make such a statement and he suggested it must mean that Nigel was about to increase their salaries.

Chuck passed the news to Bertrand that Tom had been doing his best to stop the workforce taking disruptive measures.

Another letter appeared in the *Daily Pictorial* pointing out that a joint enterprise would be difficult because French workers in aircraft factories were paid much more than their opposite numbers in England. On the strength of that letter

Tom suggested to his Production Director that the Board could increase their price to the Germans without danger of being undercut and then raise their pay in line with the French. He was told, however, that the Germans had been offered a fixed price and the only way he could expect more money was if there were fewer of them on the payroll.

"That," said Tom when he reported back to Chuck, would be "curtains for the likes of me!" Chuck looked hard at Tom and asked if he seriously believed that he and others like him were so expendable? "Nigel didn't give me to think that when I met him."

Tom groaned. "That article of yours in the *Pictorial* has really upset him. He says it's an invitation to copycats. 'Those who boast of valuables', he said, 'beckon a burglar'."

Bertrand could see he had misjudged the situation. It had been a mistake to suppose that Nigel would pay his staff more to get the work done more quickly. His ploy that Nigel would be led to think because the French paid higher wages they would be less able to undercut his prices had misfired. It was looking as though Nigel was taking it as evidence that he need no longer fear competition from the French because they were already overspending on wages. Anxious to recover the initiative, Bertrand asked to be introduced to Tom.

"I believe your wife is a school teacher" said Bernard when Tom was brought to see him.

Tom wondered what that would be leading to. "Yes, only she's on Maternity Leave at present."

"That's all right," said Bertrand. "but she taught foreign languages, didn't she? Including French?"

"Yes," said Tom, still not fathoming the drift.

"Right," said Bertrand," then do you think she'd be able to arrange a little outing for the Sixth Form in the near future?"

"I suppose so, but where to?"

"Your factory, of course," said Bertrand, and the penny dropped.

Three days later, on a fine Friday morning in the first week of June, a party of smartly dressed schoolchildren, speaking only in French, were led through the factory gates and taken to the Marketing Director's office. They were accompanied by a young teacher who had been briefed by Sara Bishop to claim he was related to the French Charge d'Affaires in London. He carried a letter which said that when they were in England the schoolchildren must visit this factory as an excellent example of British industrial enterprise.

There was a long delay while telephone calls were put through to the French Embassy who disclaimed all knowledge of the visit. The teacher pretended he must have come to the wrong place and led his hitherto well behaved group back to the factory gates. On the way, one of the boys dashed from the group, pulled out a camera and took a photograph through the open door of a hangar. He was seized by a security guard who snatched the camera and exposed the film. While this was going on another of the group rushed to a ground floor window and peered into the room. She too was seized and questioned and while the guards struggled to understand what she was saying several more of the group broke away until everyone was either running and shouting, or waving and having an argument.

Eventually the group was rounded up and the teacher signed them out at the gate as having come from Nancy, which happened to be the name of their dinner lady as well as that of the town in France known for its military connections.

When Nigel heard about the incident he was convinced the children had been spying. As a result, security at the factory was tightened. All the guards were obliged to report direct to the Managing Director at a different time each morning, to be briefed on the day's programme of expected visitors and debriefed on any unusual occurrences of the previous day. Anxious to demonstrate their improved vigilance, their first report was of a cyclist in a black beret, said to be smelling of garlic, attempting to sell onions to the Canteen Manager. The following day they described the appearance over the weekend of a number of cyclists pedalling round the perimeter of the company's airstrip wearing red, white and blue striped headgear and T-shirts advertising Pernod and Vichy Water. On Tuesday they said men from the paint shop had been seen during their lunch period throwing coloured balls into a sandpit and heard crying words like 'bule' and 'maired'.

Meanwhile reports reached the Managing Director that door-to-door salesmen and saleswomen had been calling at the homes of his executives peddling perfumes and other exotic products from heavily laden wicker baskets. Asked what was meant by 'exotic products' one director mentioned French bread, French cheese, French wines, French beans, French chalk and French polish.

Nigel was aghast. "... *And* contraceptives, I suppose!" he spluttered.

His nerves were further frayed when the local newspaper carried an advertisement appealing for aircraft engineers with a knowledge of the French language. Applicants were invited to write to a Box Number, below which was the message: *N'oubliez pas, nous vous payons bien.*

What finally convinced Nigel that all was not well was the news that a party of staff from the factory planned to spend a week-end in Paris on July 14th to join a celebration commemorating the storming of the Bastille.

The Editor of the *Daily Pictorial* received a telephone call from the Managing Director of the *Slipstream Aircraft Company.* "I am calling a Press Conference at the factory tomorrow and would like you, please, to arrange for your young reporter with an American accent to be there."

Chuck was told by the Editor to go, to stay off the liquor, and to bring back a good story.

There was no need on that occasion for Chuck to bluff his way into the M.D.'s office and his only surprise on being shown in was that he appeared to be the first to arrive.

"Hi! Come in, young man. I hope you didn't have any problems getting here today. It was good of you to come at short notice."

Chuck was puzzled by the unexpected warmth of his reception, and slightly suspicious of it. "Nice to be back!" he said, and looked around the room.

Nigel thrust a glass of champagne in his hand. "It's about the only good thing", he said, "that the French can produce these days."

Chuck ignored his editor's warning and accepted the offer. "You obviously don't think much of their aircraft, then?"

"Only ones they've copied from us, like the Concorde."

"Does that mean you think they've been copying your new design?"

"I don't know. You're a journalist, have you any better information?"

"Not really - only what I read in the papers!"

Nigel laughed. "I suppose you can get too close to the wood to see the trees." Then he told Chuck he had flown an old plane over France the previous week to look for signs of any new models the French might be making.

"Were there?"

"It was raining!"

Chuck laughed. "You don't seem to have had much luck with your Press call either. It looks like I'm the only one to have accepted."

"You're the only one I invited."

Chuck spilled his champagne.

Nigel continued. "I've thought about that trick of yours when you came to see me the first time. You know how to get things done. To get round obstacles. And you said you'd studied economics, I think."

Chuck wondered if he was about to be offered a job.

Nigel went on to describe the events that had convinced him he was being spied upon by the French. "And now", he said, "they are trying to entice the best of my staff to work for them in France."

"Who do you mean by 'them'; surely not the French government?"

"I don't know. That's what I want to find out. Which is where you come in. I'd like you to go with my staff on that trip to Paris on 14th July and to keep your ears and eyes open in case you can learn something that will help to solve the mystery. Will you do it?"

Chuck held out his glass for a refill.

"How do I fit in? Do I pretend to be a member of staff, or a stowaway, or what?"

"I suggest you go as a journalist. Gate-crash, if you like. Say you've been sent to get some more interviews to follow up the one you had with me, only this time from the other side of the boardroom. How does that strike you?"

Chuck wished he had not used that word. It reminded him that his real mission was to prevent there being … a stoppage of work.

"O.K. - but on one condition."

"Name it."

"That no-one gets victimised on the strength of anything I tell you."

"It's a deal."

They finished the bottle of Moet together and Chuck decided to avoid an early meeting with his editor.

CHAPTER 11

Paris in July is usually warm and invariably busy. Except, that is, for the weeks when everyone who can afford it goes *en vacances* to the country.

The 14th July is a national holiday and the *Slipstream* party was swept along by crowds of residents and fellow tourists, sightseeing, eating out, souvenir hunting and promenading through back streets, boulevards, museums and cafes all over the city.

Chuck had no difficulty sharing in the enjoyments while pretending to be on duty for his paper. His camera was constantly in use and his workable knowledge of the language frequently in demand. Tom Bishop performed the charade of recognising him as an old drinking pal from university and introduced him to his friends as a good guy they could rely on. Chuck, for his part, offered to give them copies of the photographs he was taking to show to their families, but suggested there might be some they would prefer not to disclose until the children were older. He did not mention the third category which he would be taking to Nigel.

Sitting with Tom and a group of his friends at a pavement cafe on the Champs Elysee, Chuck overheard some of the party talking about their jobs back home and their views on the future of the company. There was a high degree of loyalty among them, and a sense of pride in what they were about to produce, but eventually the conversation turned to the level of their wages and the prospect of better pay elsewhere. After a few glasses of Pilsner, Pernod and Napoleon brandy, pleasantries were exchanged with their French neighbours. An attempt at schoolboy French was met with a quick response in Liverpool-English, and a stream of untranslatable invective from a drunken Dutchman. Two lads from the engine assembly unit vied for the attention of a good looking woman sitting alone by the window, only to find she was German. "I am vaiting fer mine oosbant."

Some of the party succeeded in finding Parisians who were prepared to converse in broken English, or to assist them with their inadequate French, and to those heroes Chuck and Tom attached themselves, gratefully.   No-one in Paris, it seemed, had even heard of the *Slipstream Aircraft Company* and doubts were expressed at the likelihood of any aircraft company being able to survive in the present economy. By nightfall most of the party were past caring about their work, wives or wages. Some had fallen asleep by the River Seine and others abandoned sleep for the lure of a nightclub. Chuck suspected the red-light district may have captured, if not captivated, a few, but he and Tom took care to keep within the bright lights of the all-night cafes, and the safe limits of low-alcohol beer and decaffeinated coffee.

The journey home was dreadful. The sea was rough and the scene reminded Chuck of pictures he had seen of war-torn soldiers returning from the battlefront. Whether from sympathy with what he saw or what Tom called "ocean-motion", Chuck felt decidedly sick and considered his abstemious behaviour the night before had been a wasted sacrifice. Vicky met him off the boat train and greeted him with an unmistakable expression of "I might have known!" Tom's welcome from Sara was equally unsympathetic. For Chuck and Tom the pleasure of reunion was infinitely more satisfying than any pleasure experienced by their faithless or bachelor friends in a few moments of commercialised conviviality off the Place de la Concord. However, there was just a faint air of suspicion in the minds of Vicky and Sara, mixed with the aroma of *midnight madness*, when they opened the presents their husbands had bought them. Could they possibly be gifts of guilt, or were they truly the largesse of love?

Chuck's first task in the morning was to develop and print the photographs he had taken. Then, pleading the need to check up on some facts for his story, he telephoned his editor for approval to go direct to the factory where he knew Nigel would be waiting, champagne at the ready, anxious for news.

Pleasantries over, Nigel went straight to the point.

"What did you discover?"

Chuck unfastened his brief-case and pulled out the photographs.

"Quite a lot. Take a look at these." He placed a selection on Nigel's large mahogany desk.

One of them showed Jim Figures, his accountant walking out of an imposing building with a familiar looking ledger. As Chuck intended, Nigel believed it to have been a Government office but in fact it was the Bureau de Change in a large bank near the Louvre.

In the next photograph Les Rowley, his workshop superintendent, was seen clinking tankards with a pipe-smoking Frenchman at a table littered with large sheets that looked like blue-prints but were carefully smudged photo-prints of Michelin road maps.

Picture number three showed Phil Piper, his fuel supply manager, waving his wallet in the face of a man at a filling station, but what it did not show was the pump attendant standing with a nozzle at the ready.

Next he saw Charles Watchman, his security chief, arm-in-arm with a gendarme, handing over a bunch of keys - which would later be confiscated to prevent him driving off in his car.

As expected, Nigel was horrified. He stared at each picture in turn, then at the whole series. With the deftness of a card player Chuck hurriedly gathered them up and laid out another set. Nigel gasped.

First in that batch was the shot of a Frenchman (cloth cap and sharp nose) holding a copy of *Le Paris Soir* alongside a German (round face and military jacket) reading *Allgemeine Zeitung* looking furtively at each other in a cafe near the Eiffel Tower.

Next was a snapshot, much enlarged, showing Bill Steadfast, the firm's test pilot, at a fairground seated alongside a Brigitte Bardot look-alike on a flying-roundabout.

Another shot revealed a group of *Slipstream* employees on a river boat throwing paper-darts in the shape of airplanes at a passing launch.

Nigel had seen enough to be convinced his theory was right, but there was one more. Outside the German Ambassador's residence, a group of grinning revellers were seen pulling a large box-kite with the *Slipstream* company's logo clearly visible on it..

"That's it!" said Nigel. "I knew it! But what the hell do I do now? Shoot them all for treason, or fire the lot and start again?"

Chuck held back a grin. "Your men were not traitors, you know."

Nigel snapped back. "How do I know that, after all the evidence you've shown me?"

"You did say," Chuck reminded him, "that I was to keep my ears as well as eyes open."

"So?"

"Well, I did just that. On the way back I listened to people talking. Sure, they were impressed with what they saw, but I guess they were missing their fish and chips, and would rather have had a pint of beer than a glass of wine. The only reason I heard mentioned in favour of going to work in France was that the pay would be better."

"How much better?"

"Quite a lot, I guess. Of course, the figures didn't mean much to me because I don't know how much they get in English money, but it sounded a great deal more in French. ... In any case, they were calculating how long they would need to work in France to buy what an hour's work would buy over here."

"Well, what was the answer?"

"You could say France won by about four goals to three!"

Nigel took the result as he often did when his team did badly, but this time without being able to blame the referee.

"I must thank you for your help, young man, though I can't say that I like what you've brought me. You'll be paid for your efforts, of course. Just send me an invoice: time and costs. I shan't quibble, but don't overdo the expenses!"

Chuck knew it was time to go, so emptied his glass, but Nigel filled it again and made one last request.

"I'd be grateful if you didn't show your editor what you've just shown me. Do you think you could find a few less incriminating specimens from your week-end collection? And tell him I might take a page or two of advertising when we're ready to take more orders."

On his way out Chuck wondered if it had all been worth it. Sure, he had had a good week-end at someone else's expense, but he had stretched the truth to its limit and his conscience bothered him. He was brought up to believe that a lie was an act of verbal cowardice; an admission of intellectual defeat. Yeah, but the camera did not lie! It could submit the truth to more than one interpretation, as he had just shown, but that was where the eye of the beholder came in. If a senior British Civil Servant could make it fashionable to be 'economical with the truth', he was merely practising the art of being flexible with it.

By the time he reached the receptionist on the way out Chuck was aware that the effect of champagne on an empty stomach had reduced his ability to think clearly. But he did know that he ought not to sit behind the wheel of his car, so he asked if he could use the telephone. "I do actually know *how* to use it," he said, slurring his words, " P'raps I should have said *may I do so?*" The receptionist gave him an understanding smile and handed him a receiver.

Vicky was not at home when the taxi arrived, so Chuck was spared the embarrassment of explaining his extravagance. A cup of coffee, he felt, would sober him up before he faced the editor. He was asleep when Vicky returned.

Meanwhile Nigel had made up his mind what he needed to do. He summoned his Director of Production and demanded to know how long it would be before the first of the S.22's were in production?

Simon Makepiece was startled but not surprised. "Six weeks ... if there are no further set-backs."

"Too long! Make that three weeks and I'll raise everyone's wages by 30 per cent. Back-dated!"

Simon *was* now surprised. "I thought..." he began.

"Thought is past tense. Let's keep our minds on the present and look to the future. My grapevine tells me some of our workers are being wooed by the Froggies. I'm a jealous man, Simon, and I don't give way to rivals. If money will buy what I want I'll spend it! In this case, what I want will be best for all of us. The more planes we make the more we'll have to sell, and the more money we'll have to spend. So let's get on with it."

CHAPTER 12

Chuck first heard about Nigel's change of heart when he received an excited telephone call from Tom Bishop.

"It's happened," said Tom, "at last it's happened. And about bloody time! I'll bet you had something to do with it, you old blighter!"

Chuck concluded that Sara had produced the baby. Ignoring the quip about his possible involvement, he surmised the birth had been brought on by excitement following their return from Paris.

"How big is it?" Chuck asked. "Vicky will want to know."

"Nearly four thousand pounds, old boy."

"Christ! Vicky, listen to this. Wait a minute! ... Tom, talk to Vicky, she knows more about this sort of thing. I can't work it out."

The truth, of course, was no less welcome and they enjoyed the news of Tom's pay rise as much as the joke of Chuck's misunderstanding.

The eventual birth of Nigel Charles Bishop was the occasion for more celebration and Vicky and Chuck were quick to visit mother and child in a hospital ward.

After presenting Sara with flowers and the baby with a teething-ring, Vicky asked her what she would have called him if he had been a she?

"Tom was quite certain it was going to be a boy, so we never considered the alternative. I suppose Charlotte would have been all right, but Nigella might have seemed a bit contrived."

To celebrate the first off the production line of the S.22's, staff of the *Slipstream* company lined up along the factory runway and toasted its take-off with sparkling German wine poured into plastic cups. It was Nigel's way of insulting the French!

Throughout the summer months Bill Steadfast flew back and forth to Germany taking each new model as it was produced; returning by train and boat. Asked why he never came back on a commercial airline he said there was no place on an aeroplane for a back-seat driver. Nigel never went with him on any of the deliveries, which Tom said was because they were too mean to pay for the insurance.

The next big event in the lives of Tom and Sara was the christening of Nigel Charles. Chuck was invited to be a godfather but asked to be excused on the grounds that he was not sufficiently godly and didn't want a title associated with the mafia. He did, however, readily accept an invitation to the ceremony and was delighted to learn that Tom and Sara had also invited Bertrand. "If we can't have you as the child's godfather," said Tom, "we can at least have your adopted grandfather."

Christenings, like weddings, brought forth a display of new suits, smart hats and flowery buttonholes. They were occasions for extravagant hospitality, and the return of rarely seen relatives. Chuck and Vicky wished it were customary for everyone to wear name-badges or different colours to denote which side of the family they belonged to. When they were talking to strangers they often did not know if they were friends or relatives, or from which side of the family they came. When they did meet people they knew, they were subjected to jokes about how long it would be before *they* produced an excuse for another such occasion. "We're not on the same production line," Chuck told them.

Bertrand had no difficulty in making himself known. Supplied from the outset with copious helpings of champagne and other wines he revelled in the familiarity of being addressed as Old Bertie, and endeared himself to many with his Norfolk accent.

Tom had met Bertrand before and was keen to introduce him to his wife. Sara, in turn, offered to let him hold the baby. "Ah!" said Bertrand with a twinkle, "it's a rare treat to be asked. My old partner used to say it were downright careless to be left holdin' the baby, but at my age it's a pleasure."

Not so for the baby, it seemed, for young Nigel probably anticipated another dousing and emitted an irreverent scream. Bertrand, who also had fears of being wet in the process, handed the baby back to Sara.

"Don't worry, lass," he consoled her, "it's good to see the child knows who he belongs to and who's a stranger."

"I hope he won't always think of you as a stranger," said Sara, trying to make up for the baby's unfriendly behaviour.

Bertrand decided it was time to change the subject. "I have somethin' else to thank you for besides inviting me here today. I ha'n't forgot that you helped provide the cast for our little bit of French comedy at the aircraft factory."

Sara smiled. "And you helped Tom get a raise in salary, I believe."

"Let's just say, we both helped, shall we? I'm glad it worked out the way it did."

With one arm clutching her baby, Sara put the other arm through Bertrand's and steered him towards a middle-aged gentleman talking to Tom next to a table full of food and drinks. "Come with me, I'd like you to meet my headmaster...... Mr. Chalker, may I introduce Mr. Woodfellow?"

Reginald Chalker was younger than Bertrand's image of a headmaster, and Bertrand was considerably older than Mr. Chalker's image of the man who masterminded a plot to save the *Slipstream* company from a strike. He had heard about Bertrand's involvement in what Sara called 'a rescue operation' when she asked his permission to 'borrow the Sixth Form language class for a little local exercise.'

"I must congratulate you on your success as a peace-maker, but I'm afraid you may have unwittingly created a problem elsewhere." The smile on Mr. Chalker's face suggested he was teasing, but Bertrand's response was serious, and perceptive.

"It wouldn't have anything to do with your school now, would it? I thought we'd been careful to engage an incognito cast."

"Indeed you did, and thank you for that. What you did not foresee, I think, was the effect their little adventure would have on my teaching staff. You may not have known it but the morale of teachers has been getting low of late. I cannot blame them, for they complain of too much paper-work, a lack of discipline, low pay, and a poor image with the public ..."

"Oh dear, I'm very sorry. It was, I suppose, an unpaid extra chore that broke the camel's back!"

"On the contrary, my friend: yours was the event that brought life back into the French department. Unfortunately, it has made all the other departments extremely envious. You gave a new sense of purpose to people who had lost faith in what they were doing. Now all the staff want me to arrange similar exercises and I'm not sure I'll be able to help them."

Sara's glance at Bertrand, and their exchange of winks, was observed by the headmaster and his expression lightened. "I suppose you wouldn't care to ...."

Bertrand guessed what the questioner was leading up to and experienced a rare moment of panic. He could remember very little of what it was like when he went to school. He had been an inattentive pupil and his relationship with the teachers had often been hostile. When it came to his son Arthur's turn to be educated he had been more concerned with managing a workforce at his factory than listening to accounts of life in the classroom. His wife, Sally, had done that, but she was no longer alive to be consulted. From time to time he had talked to Vicky and her husband about their experience of the education system but he could never visualise what they were describing.

Aware of what seemed like an interminable silence, he told himself that a lack of first-hand knowledge had never prevented him from expressing an opinion. However, he doubted if he would make much headway with the headmaster's problem without a clearer impression of what life was like in a modern-day school.

He looked Mr. Chalker in the eye and said: "I'm a bit stale about the inside of a school: I'd need to be refreshed afore I'd be much use to you!"

"No problem there, my friend; we'll get Sara to bring you with her when she comes round with the baby."

They sealed the undertaking by clinking glasses, and spilled champagne over Sara and young Nigel.

"Oh dear, that's the second time the poor mite has been christened today! You'd better take him away from us before he develops a complex."

Bertrand looked at the headmaster and grinned. "I wonder if he liked it better than holy water?"

When Bertrand told Vicky what he had let himself in for she was less than encouraging. "Teachers are touchy people," she told him, "and they won't take kindly to you telling them what to do." Her grandfather was not easily deterred. "I never told your grandmother how to suck eggs," he said, "because I knew she made a good omelette!"

Chuck was more enthusiastic when Vicky told him what Bertrand had agreed to do. "Good! Old Bertie will make 'em sit up in the back row! He'll show 'em a few tricks they've never thought of!"

"That's what I'm afraid of," said Vicky. "He doesn't know the first thing about teaching. Morale is bad enough as it is. There are too many people telling them what they ought and ought not to do. What teachers need is support, and an occasional pat on the back."

Chuck grinned. "You'd better not tell him that, he might encourage them to pat a few backsides!"

Vicky groaned. "I'm serious, Chuck. We'd better stop him before he gets embroiled. This time he's much more likely to start a strike than to stop one."

"Have you ever tried stopping your grandfather from doing anything?"

Did they but know it, Bertrand had in fact stopped to think. He was thinking how much the world had changed since he was a boy; how much more there was to learn; and how many young people knew more than their parents did half a century ago. Many parents knew little of what their children were taught – or should have been taught.

He thought about the influence of mass-media and wondered how children ever distinguished facts from fiction. How could they be convinced of the need to study when there was so much going on that needed no instruction? By the time they left school most of them had had enough of a school environment and few of them wanted to return as teachers.

So what was it, he asked himself, that made someone like Mr. Chalker enjoy his work despite the indifference of a largely unsympathetic public? And what made him think a retired countryman, like himself, with no examinations to his credit, could contribute anything to improve the situation?

It was a challenge, he admitted, that might well defeat him, but it appealed to him that he was being asked to help people before they reached the end of their tether. Hitherto he had been confronted with situations that were already out of hand and on the verge of disruption. Here he would be looking for ways of revitalising interest in a job that had just become dull and devalued.

He resolved to accept the challenge.

Fred C. Gee

CHAPTER 13

It was early in September, soon after the start of a new term, when Bertrand arrived at the *Larkwood School* with Sara and her three month old son, Nigel. Sara found it strange to be going back as a visitor after two years on the staff, but her pride at showing off the baby masked any inclination to resume her old duties as a teacher. Neither was there any inclination on Bertrand's part to return as a pupil, except insofar as he had come to learn something about what was now being taught to a younger generation.

His first reaction on passing through the gates was to wonder why it was necessary to fence the place in and whether the eight-foot high iron railings were meant to restrain the children from escaping or to protect them from intruders. No wonder his recollections of schooldays were of captivity and frustration rather than lessons and enlightenment!

Beyond the gate, between railings and classrooms, was an expanse of tarmac, patterned with white and yellow lines, which he took at first to be a car park but then recognised was the playground. Less familiar were the group of huts huddled in a corner of the play area which Sara said were 'portaloos'. Closer inspection showed that one was labelled BOYS and the other GIRLS. There were no cryptic symbols such as mystified him in the *Bricklayers Arms* at Stillborough.

Force of habit led Sara to park her perambulator in the bicycle shed and to carry Nigel into the school by the door reserved exclusively for STAFF. Bertrand followed and found himself in a narrow corridor that opened into a lobby where two upholstered chairs and a small low table formed a reception area. On the wall in front of the chairs was a hatch over which were written the words SCHOOL OFFICE, the last three letters having at some time in the past been obliterated: a fact made obvious by the unconvincing attempt to replace them.

Sara pressed the bell and a glass panel moved sideways to reveal a middle-aged lady with a permanent expression of "not-today-thank-you". When she saw Sara, however, she threw the glass panel back to its limit and called out in a loud voice: "It's Sara, and ... Oh, isn't he lovely!" A stable door, below the hatch, was thrown open and mother and child were whisked inside - to the amusement of Bertrand who was ignominiously overlooked. Left alone in the lobby, he took the opportunity to wander along the corridor and had just reached a door marked PRIVATE when it opened and a smart, well-built lady in her late twenties stepped out. On seeing Bertrand she stopped abruptly. "Oh, I'm so sorry," she said, "you must be Mr. Woodfellow."

"Yes Madam," said Bertrand, "but don't apologise. That is my misfortune, not yours!"

Miss Beecham blushed. "Mr. Chalker is expecting you. Please come this way." She led Bertrand through an outer office to the Headmaster's room.

"Come in, Bertie, old man," said the Head in his heartiest manner. "Welcome to *Larkwood*. Delighted to see you. Does it bring back memories?"

Bertrand was not sure how to answer that, or how to respond to the familiarity. "The last time I were shown into a headmaster's office were to get six o' the best!"

"Well, we don't do that sort of thing now, you know. But I can offer you some coffee out of our best china! Miss Beecham won't mind making some, I'm sure; will you Polly?"

Miss Beecham was still smarting under Bertrand's repartee when they met in the corridor and avoided giving him any further cause to comment.

"Now then," said Mr. Chalker, "before Polly returns let us decide how we are to explain your presence to the staff. I take it you still wish to have an alibi?"

"Yes. I think that's the best idea. After all, it's your ship and I'll be what you might call a stowaway!"

"I hope that doesn't mean you'll want to hide out in our cupboards!"

"Ah now, that might be necessary! I hadn't thought of it but perhaps if I did I'd learn what really goes on here."

"You would learn how hard up we are for books and equipment. Most of our cupboards are bare."

Polly returned and overheard the mention of cupboards and hiding. It was clear that she doubted if Bertrand would fit in a school cupboard. "Do you take sugar, Mr. Woodfellow?" she asked, and felt better now that she had made that observation. She filled their cups and retired to her room.

Bertrand turned to the headmaster and they resumed their discussion. "I suppose you could tell the staff I'm looking for a job as a gardener."

"Surely not! Not if you want them to take you seriously. A school governor, perhaps, but not a gardener."

"Governor sounds a bit too ... well, too official; like I was here to check up on them."

"How about a parent, then? Or a prospective parent?"

"Maybe, except they might think 'the old boy's a bit past it', if you see what I mean."

"*That's it*! You've got it! You're an Old Boy, back from the past to look over his old school. On a trip to the land of Nostalgia."

Bertrand shared the headmaster's relief at finding that solution, and privately welcomed the compliment, having come from a less auspicious school in the country. He finished his coffee and was taken by Mr. Chalker to the Staff Room just as the bell was ringing for the mid-morning break.

It was a thoroughly untidy room, with half-filled ash trays on tables, arm chairs and window sills; newspapers and journals strewn around the floor over threadbare carpets; raincoats, overalls and sweaters flung across the backs of upright chairs; an assortment of dirty cups, mugs and glasses with empty cans of soft drinks and coca cola; the atmosphere polluted by smoke and stale air. Accustomed to all this, and the usual noise of conversation, the headmaster was unprepared as he opened the door for the sound of a baby crying. He then remembered the arrangement by which Sara was to take Bertrand with her when she came to introduce young Nigel to her old workmates.

"Good morning, everybody," he boomed, standing in the doorway. "This is quite a unique occasion. Today we have the pleasure of welcoming not only the youngest new boy to *Larkwood*, who I see you have already met, but also a very distinguished Old Boy, Mr. Bertrand Woodfellow." News of the presence of young Nigel had spread through the school more quickly than any mention of Bertrand. Sara Bishop had been a popular teacher and she was remembered with affection by most of those she taught. All the girls, without exception, and most of the boys, were curious to see the child that was the cause of her recent absence. As soon as the break was over she took her baby on a tour of the classrooms, interrupting lessons to everyone's delight.

Bertrand, meantime, remained in the Staff Room talking to those teachers who had what was euphemistically called a Rest Period. He told them he had been busy in business for a very long time and had forgotten all he ever learned at school. Now that he had retired, he said, he wanted to be reminded of his school days so he could include them in memoirs he was about to write.

It was a revelation that came to him on the spur of the moment and it left his audience as impressed as if he had been a film star.

Having thus established his alibi, Bertrand set off to catch up with Sara and Nigel on their tour of the school so that he could be shown into some of the classrooms they would be visiting and talk to more of the teachers. As they progressed, he observed many of the changes that had taken place since he was a boy and felt for the first time that maybe he had been born a generation too soon.

Teachers, he noticed, no longer wore gowns and their pupils were not regimented to file in and out of classrooms as he was made to do. Classroom furniture looked decidedly more practical and comfortable than he remembered it, for he could see none of the long backless forms on which he and his classmates used to sit, and there wasn't an ink well in sight. Gone too were the blackboards on easels, replaced by large movable boards that slid over each other when they were filled.

He looked with envy at the spacious laboratories with their smart metallic sinks and long benches fitted with water taps and gas burners; at the special rooms for wood and metal working, for music making, and for viewing films and television programmes. There was a large gymnasium with all manner of sports and exercise equipment, and an indoor swimming pool.

The library was not just a collection of books arranged on shelves, but a place where children could sit quietly and read; and it was equipped with a photocopier and something called a micro-fiche reader.

At lunch time he saw tables set in the Assembly Hall and meals being served to those who could not or did not want to go home for them.

It all resembled an exclusive club house, and Bertrand wondered how the teachers could possibly be discontented. What was it, he wondered, that was missing, or what malevolent influence could be making them dissatisfied.

He compared in his mind the poor state of the Staff Room with the relative richness of the classroom facilities and felt it ought to be telling him something. There was no time left to discuss such matters but he resolved to return to them later.

There was, however, time that evening for him to talk to Vicky and Chuck about what he had seen, for he had arranged to spend the night with them in Blixford rather than go back to Trimstead. Vicky was still critical of his meddling in what she called the modern approach to learning and protested that he ought to confine himself to problems about which he had first-hand knowledge. That amused Bertrand who reminded her that he was at school before she was born and since then had experience of meeting many unsatisfactory products of the education system.

Chuck had a different reason for lacking enthusiasm for Bertrand's latest enterprise. He could see nothing in it for him.

"Guess you're on your own with this one, gran'pa," he muttered. "Can't see much scope in it for a guy with a camera."

"You might be wrong about that, young man," said Bertrand. "If I'm not mistaken there'll be quite a few stories worth illustrating before the school term is over. You mark my words."

Chuck scoffed and marked him two out of ten for his effort so far.

Bertrand devoted all the following day at *Larkwood School* to getting to know the teachers. There was no question of them 'marking his words' for he did little of the talking. He was content to listen to what they had to say. They were all professional story-tellers and each had a similar story to tell. In pantomime language, they were either Cinderellas or Buttons, and they had yet to meet the Fairy Godmother who could dress them in fine clothes and transport them to a Ball. The Ugly Sisters appeared to be H.M.I.s and the Wicked Baron was clearly identified as the Secretary of State for Education. Somewhere in the scenario there should have been parts for the children, but the impression Bertrand got was that their role was merely that of dispassionate spectators.

CHAPTER 14

Evelyn Wordsmith was the English teacher and she had arranged for Bertrand to call on her at the end of a lesson. He slipped quietly into the classroom, noticed only by those in the back row, and their attention quickly reverted to the front as one of them was called upon to answer a question.

"John. '*Look to the lady*'... Who said that?"

"You did, Miss."

"And who else?"

"Shakespeare?"

"Oh, you have been listening, then?"

"Macbeth?"

"You're guessing. Try Macduff."

"Please Miss..." A hand went up.

"Banquo said it."

"So did Macduff. Sometimes, you see, there is more than one answer to a question. Perhaps we should remember that occasionally."

Bertrand felt strangely at home. They were reading Shakespeare when he was a boy. Somehow he had expected Evelyn to be taking them through a book by Margaret Drabble, or Iris Murdoch, or perhaps Patricia Highsmith. He wondered if Macbeth had been brought in specially for his benefit but could see from the condition of the books that they had been in regular use for a long time. He made a mental note to ask what modern authors they had studied and was pleased to hear Evelyn close the lesson by asking for an essay comparing Macbeth with any book they had been reading recently.

The burst of noise and rush for the doors as the class was dismissed reminded Bertrand of his workers' response to the factory hooter at the end of their working day. Evelyn apologised, but saw from Bertrand's smile that he was pleased and sympathetic. She commented on the difficulty of overcoming external influences, like parents and the media, and said it was hard to convey the importance of words and sentence construction when there was so little interest in such matters at home.

"Getting children to spell correctly is a constant struggle. That's why I insist on them reading aloud and looking at each word on the page. If I had the money I'd see they each had a dictionary on their desk. And writing is another problem which can't be left to solve itself. Too many of them come up from the Junior School unprepared for the amount of writing they'll have to do as they get older. When I see a child pressing on a pen or pencil - or a biro - as if it were a garden spade I wince. Think of the energy they'll waste, and how hard it will be to keep up with the speed of their thoughts."

Bertrand agreed, but detected an attempt to impress him. Before she could unleash another hobby-horse he pulled on the reins by asking her the question uppermost in his mind. "If I were your Fairy Godmother, what would you ask for?"

Evelyn laughed. She could overlook the misplaced gender, but could not resist the temptation to point out that the word 'fairy' had a connotation which might not have been prevalent when he was at school. Bertrand was glad to know she was not as stuffy as he had begun to suspect, and even happier when she told him her greatest wish was to provide the next generation with more people who valued their language and were prepared to support those who taught it.

He thanked her for their meeting and moved on to the neighbouring classroom where Adrian Sommers was about to begin a lesson in mathematics. Known to the school as Old Adder, he was by no means old and in no way restricted his teaching to arithmetic, but he was proud of the nickname because, he said, it meant he was no ordinary snake-in-the-grass: adders, he said, could bite! Bertrand felt a warmth towards the man but, unlike his previous call, found little in the lesson to remind him of his own experience.

Aware of a visitor, and unsure of his importance, the boys and girls went quietly to their desks, assuming expressions of mock attentiveness. Adrian went straight to the blackboard and began to fill it with numbers. The numbers themselves were familiar enough (there were, after all, only nine of them; ten if you included zero,) but Bertrand wondered why they were being arranged in boxes with strange signs and inexplicable symbols. Confused, he turned his attention to a textbook on the desk next to where he was sitting. Words like *matrices, topology* and *cybernetics* appeared and there were pages devoted to *sets* and *games*. He looked again at the cover, thinking he might have picked up a book about tennis. Meanwhile most of the class had turned away from the blackboard. Some were glancing at pages held below their desks in a manner suggesting they were probably not mathematical. Others were talking to their neighbours. Bertrand shared their relief when the lesson ended.

Adrian sensed it and asked if his visitor had much to do with numbers during his working life. Bertrand hesitated before answering.

"When I were a carpenter," he said, "I had to measure, and sometimes to multiply; and as a manager I had to do accounts and calculate profit, but math'matics for me has always meant arithmetic. I did do geometry, I suppose, when I was making or designing things, but I never used algebra or trig'o'nometry and I never understood log'rythms or calc'lus. But then, I never needed 'em. Of course, I know now they're a must for engineers and scientists but they were always a 'turn off' when I were at school. Now we have pocket calculators maybe they aren't so important."

Adrian assured him such subjects had still to be taught. "I agree the computer has taken the chore out of number crunching but I never know who in the class will want to be an engineer or scientist so I have to treat them all alike."

Fearing he might attempt to condense a year's syllabus into the next ten minutes, Bertrand thanked him for his hospitality and turned to leave.

"If you would like to come again tomorrow," said Adrian, "my subject will be 'Probability and an Introduction to Statistics'."

"Damn lies, eh?" said Bertrand with a friendly grin.

"Probably!" said Adrian with a sigh.

There was one more lesson before lunch and Bertrand had arranged to sit in on Chemistry. His recollection of that subject conjured up images of coloured flames over gushing bunsen burners and an elderly teacher in acid-stained overall, known irreverently as Old Stinker. It was something of a shock, therefore, to be greeted in the laboratory by a twenty-two year old female in a spotlessly clean lab coat standing between rows of brightly polished benches and keenly occupied comfortable-looking stools.

"Good morning, sir."

Bertrand looked round, then realised the greeting was directed at him by the teacher.

"G'd morning ... er ... do I say, Miss?"

"Call me Lucy, the others do. They think it's short for Lucifer, but I don't mind."

"Thanks. I hope I'm not a disruptive influence."

"Do you want to join in, or just watch?"

"Goodness-me, I wouldn't know where to start! I'd probably blow you all up if I tampered with those taps and that apparatus."

After a while Lucy Dalton detached herself from the experimenters and drew up a stool to sit beside Bertrand at the end of a bench. She quizzed him fiercely about his interest in what she was doing and told him bluntly that she assumed he was there as a government or political spy. This amused Bertrand who thought she was likely to explode if tampered with and, knowing the best form of defence was attack, he asked her how she came to be a teacher of chemistry.

"Are you interested in why I teach, or why I teach chemistry?"

"I were just thinking, it wouldn't ha' been a suitable subject for a lady at one time."

"Hadn't your generation ever heard of Marie Curie?"

"Ah, well! Yes, I suppose they had. But X-rays were a bit of a mystery then, and mysterious women weren't thought to be right company for us kids!"

"When you asked the question did you regard me as mysterious?"

"No. But maybe I do now."

Lucy laughed. "I doubt if anyone else in Larkwood thinks that. Do you really want to know why I took up teaching?"

"Certainly."

Lucy obliged ... at length! She told him she wanted to be a scientist, because while she was at school she heard they were in short supply. Then, while she was at university working for her degree she found there was a recession on and it was jobs that were in short supply. When she asked herself why there was a recession she came to the conclusion it was because there weren't enough people trained to *make* things. That, she thought, might have been because the right subjects weren't being taught in schools, or because the teachers were more interested in getting students into universities than to factories and workshops.

"So", she said, "I made up my mind to be a teacher, to help get the country out of recession. I daresay you think that was conceited of me, or was I just naive?"

Bertrand assured her he thought no such thing.

"I can tell you now, it was bloody stupid of me!"

Bertrand pretended to be shocked.

"I had the silly idea that once the government realised they needed more trained technicians and scientists they would make it worth our while to go into teaching instead of accountancy or public relations. After all, they believed in market forces and value for money. Instead I found they treated all State School teachers as left-wing layabouts and only those who taught in the private sector got a decent salary."

Bertrand smiled. "Do I detect just a tiny chip on that tender shoulder of yours?"

"No. It's a bloody big chip! I feel I've been cheated and the kids are being robbed."

Bertrand listened while she expounded her argument.

The country was not short of talent, she said, but talents were being wasted. Money was going into the hands of people who left school with no interest in education, and not nearly enough was going back to cultivate the skills of the next generation. A nation that led the world in banking and investment had failed to support and invest in its youth. While other countries, our competitors, fed their schools and colleges with funds and held their teachers and scholars in high regard, we expected ours to fend for themselves. And, daftest of all, she added, in the midst of depression we expected industry and commerce, whose profits were falling, to sponsor and subsidise the schools and colleges.

There was no time left for Bertrand to gain an impression of how Lucy was teaching chemistry, but he had gained a very good idea of how she felt about the state of her profession. By the time the lesson ended he wondered why they needed those burners on the bench when there was so much fire in her belly. It was cooler in the canteen where she took him for lunch.

Conversation over cottage-pie, peas and chips was as conventional as the meal. There were comments on the weather, current sporting events and the latest television comedy, but nothing directly concerned with the school or anything to do with the subject of education.

Asked if his presence was inhibiting them from talking 'shop' Lucy replied. "We've decided not to work in our rest periods, or over lunch, until we're paid and treated like professionals. You'd call it working-to-rule, I suppose."

Bertrand did not say what he would call it but tried to change the mood.

"If the word gets around," he said. "you might find the kitchen staff will follow suit."

Adrian nodded. "I think they have already. Why else have we got cottage pie? Once upon a time it would have been steak-and-kidney!"

They were led by this recollection to talk about the good old days at *Larkwood School* when teaching was fun and the children were more often obedient than otherwise. Bertrand was too long in the tooth to swallow that, but again decided not to contradict. Memories, he knew, were a mixture of fact and fantasy. Appropriately his next visit was to a history lesson.

There was a distinctly changed atmosphere about the school during the afternoon. The effect of 'school dinners' and incipient fatigue had been to slow the tempo and increase what Stephen Godwin, the history teacher, called 'the yawn factor'. Stephen was a man in his late twenties who had already lost most of the enthusiasm for teaching with which he started out. Few of the children at *Larkwood* had shown any interest in history, which they heard say was 'bunk', and Stephen said if five percent of them were to go on to study the subject at university it would be a record. There were, he added, only two outlets for those who persisted: one was the Civil Service and the other Teaching.

Stephen felt he had probably chosen the wrong option, and Bertrand was made aware of that when he entered the classroom.

"I don't want to be rude, Mr. Woodfellow, but I doubt if much has changed since you were here as far as my subject is concerned. You'd probably learn more about world history sitting in a barber's shop."

"Oh, come now! Much has happened since I were at school so history can't be just about 1066, and the Wars of the Roses. I'm sure you're more up to date than that."

"Oh, sure! We have journalists to give us the outcome of events before they even happen. Yes, we're always up to date. But is that history? The moment I mention a place or a person connected with some great historical event, everyone here thinks they know about it from what they have seen on television or in the cinema. They don't want my version."

Bertrand was wondering how to console the man, when Stephen offered him an unexpected opportunity. "I suppose you wouldn't like to take the lesson this afternoon and give them some first-hand material, would you?"

Bertrand was taken aback. It suddenly dawned on him that to this young man, and more so the children in front of him, *he* was now history. They were not born when he was their age. The world he knew as a boy was further away from them than the turn of the century had been to Bertrand when he was at school.

'Old Bertie' was a great success. His anecdotes about the war and the following years of austerity were followed by stories of how he listened to news on the radio before there was television and what a thrill it was when England won the World Cup at football. To change the mood he made them laugh by telling them he once played truant and was chased by a bull, ending up at the top of a haystack.

"You won't find that story in your history books," he told them, "and you won't get that sort o' kick sittin' in front of a television set!"

As he hurried down the corridors to a Geography lesson Bertrand reflected on the experience he had just enjoyed: the pleasure of communicating with a responsive audience, the intoxication of being appreciated. It was the emotion felt by an actor or a politician, a clergyman or a successful salesman. He had just sensed the attractive side of teaching, and could now imagine the contrasting misery when those sensations were absent.

Geography was the province of Gwyneth Snowdon, a native of the Welsh valleys and an excellent disciplinarian. Sweet of voice and strong of arm, she conducted her lessons as she would a choir and her displeasure as she would at a rugby match. Her pupils had learned to stay in tune and keep their heads down, but harmony was won at the expense of enterprise and few of them got good marks in their examinations.

Bertrand was hardly in the classroom before she tackled him. "What you have here", she told him, "is a group of disorientated, disenchanted children who regard geography as something the travel agents thought up to promote holidays abroad. The only time I ever see them interested is when one of them comes back from a package tour with a load of photographs. There was a time," she added without pausing for breath, "when I could take them on field trips and foreign visits, but the Education Office has stopped all that and the nearest we get to three dimensional landscapes is plotting contours from a Survey map. You are welcome to stay and watch while I try to enthuse them about earthquakes and volcanoes, but I warn you it won't be a very shattering experience."

"I'll stay, if you don't mind, but please don't let me disturb you."

The more he thought about it while Gwyneth was taking the lesson, the more he realised it was she who was disturbing him. Of all the lessons he had attended that day the one he would have expected to be the most popular and easily assimilated was geography. Instead it was dull and rambling; delivered in a silence so cold that lava from the volcano would

The Trouble With Grandpa

not have warmed the atmosphere. Was it, he wondered, the subject or the teacher he had failed to understand? Or was it the teacher who failed to understand and reach her audience?

Bertrand was glad to move on to the last lesson of the day.

A great noise was coming from the gymnasium as he approached. It was not the discordant mixing of juvenile voices such as would come from an unruly classroom but a melodic crescendo of musical instruments belonging to the school orchestra. Seated in a semi-circle before a stout lady waving her arms was a group of fifth and sixth formers cheerfully practising for a performance to be given on the School Prize Day at the end of term. Bertrand beat time with his feet and applauded when they finished. There was no sign of disenchantment in that department.

"Marvellous," said Bertrand. "We only had a drum and a recorder when I was at school."

"That's how it will be again if this government has its way. We've no budget for new or replacement instruments and my post will be downgraded when I retire at the end of this year. That's what our politicians think of a subject that has universal appeal and the ability to make people happy. It makes me so angry I could wish them all *deaf*."

"Perhaps they are already," said Bertrand feeling that way himself. This lady, he decided, deserved encouragement. "I *also* think that making people happy is better than making them rich."

He overstepped the mark.

"There's nothing wrong with being rich. It's being ignorant that makes me mad. How can they claim the right to rule a country when they refuse to invest in its talent?"

It had been a long day, and Bertrand had much to think about.

CHAPTER 15

Reginald Chalker rose from his chair to greet Bertrand as he entered the headmaster's study.

"Well, Mr. Woodfellow what did it feel like to be back at school again yesterday?"

"Depressing," said Bertrand, who had spent most of the night wondering how to answer the inevitable question. It was not the answer Mr. Chalker expected. He waited for the explanation.

"I think I understand why you asked me to look around."

"Do you, now? I rather hoped you'd tell me I was wrong."

"For a time I thought you were. Then I began to get the feeling all was not well. By the end of the afternoon I was sure it wasn't. Morale is decidedly low. What you said about being short of books and equipment is true enough, but I don't think shortages lie at the root of your problem. I'd say you need to look deeper than that. All the teachers I met were quite capable of coping with what little they'd got. I suspect they are unhappy because something else is missing."

"Go on, I'm listening."

"I think your staff feel the lack of public respect. They sense that parents ... politicians ... journalists ... Civil Servants ... undervalue their work ... see them as a fixture ... take them for granted. It's robbed them of self-esteem and they resent it."

"Was it any different when you were at school?"

"Well, yes, I think it was. In those days teachers were looked upon as responsible people, like policemen and bank managers and civil servants. But now, all those careers have been devalued by bad publicity and by the media. Anyone who has any claim to authority these days is automatically debunked."

The headmaster was fidgeting with his paper knife. He pointed it quizzically at Bertrand.

"Do you think the staff here will try to do anything about it?"

"I did hear talk in one quarter of working-to-rule."

"You don't have to tell me who that was. I'll wager it was our young Chemistry mistress."

"Dear me! Is Miss Dalton that transparent? She struck me as a very capable teacher."

"Oh yes, she's capable all right. Capable of doing almost anything. Organising a strike, for example. She likes to live up to her nickname. Did she tell you her name was short for Lucifer?"

"Yes, she did, as a matter of fact."

"And what do you know about Lucifer?"

"Only what I looked up in a book last night. It was all Greek to me! But I gather it has something to do with the Morning Star."

"I hadn't thought of that connection! There's another definition in my dictionary. 'Leader of the rebellion of angels,' it says, and 'usually identified with Satan'. That just about says it all."

"Mmm! She's a bit of a devil then by the sound of it?"

"Well, what do *you* think? You heard her talking about working-to-rule."

"I wouldn't blame her particularly. She's only expressing the feelings of others. I've told you what they think and, I'm afraid, I'm inclined to agree with them."

Mr. Chalker hesitated for a minute, then swivelled the paper knife until it pointed to himself.

"Would it surprise you if I said I do too?"

"Well, good for you! Now, the question is, can we do something about it?"

"I'm glad you said 'we'. I'm ready to take advice, but I am probably too near the trees to see the wood as you may see it. Now that you have had a closer look, perhaps you can suggest a way out."

Bertrand made his position clear. He could not, he said, offer any suggestions about the content of lessons or the manner in which subjects were taught. They were matters for the headmaster to address. He would confine himself, he said, to ways in which he thought the teaching staff should try to influence local opinion. They must make everyone in the neighbourhood aware of what was happening to the school. There was an election coming up and they must try to shame the electors into wanting something better for their children.

"I know it won't be easy," Bertrand said, "because there aren't many votes in education for ambitious politicians. Too few of the voters will have had much of an education themselves and most of 'em don't see a need for it."

"You could also say that about the politicians, could you not," said Mr. Chalker.

"Too true," said Bertrand, imitating the style of a politician, "but our aim just now is to restore the morale of teachers at *Larkwood School*."

"Hear, hear!" said the headmaster and rang for some coffee.

Miss Beecham was now relaxed in her dealings with Bertrand and she handed him his cup with a smile. "I expect you wish you were young again," she added as she offered him a biscuit. Mr. Chalker would have considered that impertinent from anyone else, but was delighted to find her warming towards his visitor.

"Mr. Woodfellow is still very young at heart, don't you think, Polly. I doubt if I shall be as vigorous by the time I retire."

Bertrand enjoyed the flattery. "It's the young who make you young, is what I say".

Polly wondered if he thought she was looking younger, or older, than she really was, and left before any more was said. When she had gone, the men got down to business and began to discuss ways of improving staff morale.

Bertrand suggested the first step the headmaster could take would be to raise their spirits at the start of the day. "I saw teachers coming through the gate this morning with expressions like they'd just been beaten up over breakfast. Couldn't we cheer 'em up a bit? Instead of sounding that old brass bell to call them to assembly, why don't you use your tannoy and play a good old Sousa march, or something like it, to liven 'em up?"

Mr. Chalker made a note on the pad in front of him, frowning a little at first, then woke to the possibilities. "I'll ask Miss Belton to organise it - starting tomorrow."

Bertrand pressed home the idea. "It won't do to repeat the same tunes too often, like they do in restaurants and supermarkets. There's a piece my family plays on a record by a chap called ... pro- ... coffee, or something like that ..."

"Prokoviev?"

"That's him. It gets me moving, I can tell you!"

Another note went on the pad, and Mr Chalker waited for the next suggestion.

"On special days you could have the school orchestra playing live."

Mr. Chalker did not make a note of that; but he had got the message. "We'll leave all that to Miss Belton, shall we? Who's next on your list?"

"The public. We must get them on your side, and the best way to do that is to go out after them. I've got several ideas, but they must all appear to come from you. Let's talk about them first and if you like them you can set the staff to work on them."

After listening to several examples Mr. Chalker was doubtful, at first, whether Bertrand's ideas would appeal to the public but he thought they would amuse the staff and that would help to improve their morale, if only temporarily. He told Bertrand he would hold a Special Staff Meeting that afternoon, 'to test the water'.

"In that case, don't put it to 'em cold. Try warming them up a bit first. Tell them you've learned - from an unimpeachable source - that the school has been picked to feature in a newspaper series about how the youth of today are educated."

Mr. Chalker raised his eyebrows.

Bertrand took from his pocket a crumpled up copy of the *Daily Pictorial*, pointed to a picture which Chuck had taken, and dropped it on the desk. "With your permission," he said, "it can be arranged."

On the way out, Bertrand put his head round Miss Beecham's door.

"Thanks for the coffee."

Before she could pull herself together to say she never meant to offend him, Bertrand had gone.

Special Staff Meetings at *Larkwood* were usually occasions for announcing bad or uncomfortable news so when one was called by Mr. Chalker the expectation of most staff members was that further cuts were about to be made. The appearance of the Head with a smile on his face seemed to confirm that suspicion, but they were pleasantly surprised, indeed astonished, when he invited them to join him in a campaign to clean up the image of the schoolteacher. "It will involve you," he said, "in taking to the streets and possibly washing your linen in public. You must capture the attention of every citizen; seize the imagination of passers-by; win the acclaim of shopkeepers......."

"Is this another out-of-school exercise you have in mind, headmaster?"

"Are we being asked to demonstrate in support of the government?"

"Or against it?"

"Is this to be voluntary, or shall we be having new terms of employment?"

"Have you not been feeling too well lately, headmaster?"

Mr. Chalker listened to their questions with amusement and then proceeded to explain in detail what he had in mind.

They would each be able to choose when and where they made their contribution; even whether they joined in or not. What he hoped would happen was that they would get as much benefit and enjoyment from whatever they did as Sara Bishop's Sixth Form got from their outing to the aircraft factory. If it brought a little fun back into their lives, he said, it could save them all from coronaries.

No-one in the Staff Room could fail to respond on those terms and they all returned to their homes that evening lighter of heart than for a very long time.

Back in Trimstead that evening Bertrand telephoned a message to Chuck alerting him to some photographic opportunities he could expect soon in the vicinity of Larkwood.

The following morning teachers were queuing up by the headmaster's office to discuss ways of implementing his proposed campaign. Polly Beecham was overwhelmed, and dying to know what the headmaster could possibly have told them to create such interest. Mr. Chalker's dilemma was to decide whether or not to influence what each teacher might want to do, and whether to set a schedule to spread the impact over a definite period or let them go simultaneously to create the maximum effect. One thing he had to make clear was that there would be no more money in the kitty from which to finance whatever they had in mind.

The inhabitants of Larkwood were a sober community accustomed to going about their daily routines in a quiet and peaceful way. The streets were busier with motor traffic than they used to be, but the pavements were generally uncluttered by pedestrians. There was a short flurry in the morning when commuters were rushing for their bus to the county town, and again in the evening when they returned home; and the occasional trail of children ambling or scurrying to and from school, but local shoppers tended to spread their journeys over wider routes and longer intervals and tourists were few enough to be virtually unnoticed.   It came as a shock, therefore, to those who frequented the neighbourhood, to find the town suddenly drenched with children pouring over the pavements and grouping into clusters round their teachers in hitherto deserted places.

Miss Snowdon was out with her fifth form geographers, mapping the district with meticulous precision. Measurements were taken, with theodolites on tripods and tapes strewn along the pavements, then plotted on maps. People strolled by and stepped round or over the obstructions, smiled and grumbled but rarely stopped ... or understood.

Close by, in the Car Park, youngsters with notebooks and pencils were shouting excitedly across the tops of cars, while they collected registration numbers and recorded the make, model and colour of all the vehicles they could see. Urging them on, Mr. Sommers stood like a ticket inspector waiting to collect fines from the absent drivers.

Eager pupils in Mr Godwin's history class, armed with miniature tape recorders, were busy inviting elderly passers-by to talk about their memories of what life was like when they were young.

With even greater enthusiasm Miss Wordsmith led her English class to the Public Library where normally silence was as much preserved as books and periodicals. Suddenly it became a boisterous bidding chamber as a crowd of sixth formers swarmed among the shelves, calling out titles and looking for unfamiliar authors like Dostoevsky and Turgenev. Coats and scarves were flung across chairs, and books scattered among the tables to be read. Notes were made and loudly discussed as their teacher moved from one to another, answering their questions. A distraught librarian called for assistance as the decibel level rose to unheard of heights. A lonely member of the public dropped the newspaper he was reading and fled for solitude to the loo.

Another sanctum where silence was normally the order of the day was the Church of St.Christopher. Situated near the centre of the town the church was surrounded by a concrete courtyard with a fountain and neighbouring gardens. A feature of the church was its tall and majestic clock tower with a castellated roof from which one could see for miles around. Never before had so many feet climbed the spiral staircase in such quick succession. The remainder of Mr Newton's Physics class who were left below then saw bodies hanging over the parapet like wilting stems in a vase. They stared up from the courtyard waiting to measure the time it took various articles to fall from the tower. One boy held a stop-watch, another a notebook and a third one called out the moment he saw the article being dropped and again as it hit the ground. Galileo had done it before, but no-one else had ever done it in Larkwood.

Half a mile away, in the Paradise Gardens, an orchestra was playing in the bandstand. Initially there was no audience, for the publicised concerts were at week-ends and public holidays, but once the sound of music had drifted across the beds of dahlias and delphiniums, people were drawn from afar and the seats that stood empty around the arena filled rapidly. Waving rhythmically from the rostrum, delighted with her performers, Miss Belinda Belton was beating out the time of her life.

CHAPTER 16

History was made at *Larkwood School* on the morning after the headmaster's experiment in street-wise practicals. Every one of the teachers and all the boys and girls reported for school on time. At five minutes to nine, instead of late-comers arriving to the last echoes of a brass bell, the entire school marched in to Assembly with a swagger and smile to the sound of a brass band playing a tune called 'Children of the Regiment'. The reason for this unique display of punctuality was an eagerness to report back on the previous day's exercise.

Mr. Chalker led his teachers on to the platform. Beaming at Miss Belton, he acknowledged her appropriate and excellent choice of music, and announced to the assembled company his satisfaction at the response to his call for action. Pointing to Miss Snowdon he said he believed it had helped to put the school back on the map.

He waited for a laugh and then turned to Miss Dalton who was standing beside him: "Tomorrow we must carry the torch of learning into the heart of the community until a flame burns brightly in the homes of all those who value art and knowledge. We must then see to it that the light does not go out, for our future will depend upon the support we get from the man-in-the-street... and, of course, the woman ... the women ... the men and women, who pay taxes ... the people who vote and elect those who decide our share of the wealth."

A loud cough from the deputy head stemmed the flow of Mr. Chalker's rhetoric, but did not stop it entirely.

"Now," he added, "is the moment for us to cash in on the fact that an election is coming. We must make the voters aware of our existence, of our inadequate resources, and our determination to stand up and be counted. It is," he cried, raising the pitch of his voice to indicate the imminence of conclusion, "no longer necessary for you to be seen and not heard. You must go out there and be seen *and heard*."

There were loud cheers and more noise from the vigorous stamping of feet.

"I should rest your feet, if I were you," he called, "for you'll be needing them again this afternoon."

To which there were boos – followed by a lot of laughter.

Talk in the Staff Room was dominated by anecdotes of the previous day's events. Of the lady who thought they were throwing discarded clothing from the clock tower of the church and that a suicide was about to be committed; of the elderly gentleman who wanted to talk about his amorous adventures in a field where the police station now stood; and of the couple they found flirting in the back of a Vauxhall when they were counting the number of cars in the car park.

Not all the teachers had taken part in the 'exercises', and Miss Dalton was one who expressed doubts about their value. She argued that the only way they would make the public aware of their existence was to withhold their labour and force parents to keep their children at home. Nothing had yet persuaded her to change her mind, but the opportunity to get out in the fresh air and have some fun was too good to miss and she cheerfully volunteered to go at the next opportunity.

Mr. Sommers's class of young mathematicians returned to the car park to get more data for statistical analysis, and Miss Snowdon's geographers resumed work on up-dating the local street map. The history class continued to interview senior citizens and extended its targets to include passengers on buses and businessmen in offices. Introductions to retired doctors and solicitors were followed up out of school hours and Mr Godwin realised he had enough material to fill a book. The English class went back to the library where they commandeered the stock of newspapers in order to read leading articles and obituaries - with the promise of a prize from Miss Wordsmith for whoever found the largest number of misprints, spelling mistakes and grammatical errors. Unable to occupy the municipal bandstand for a second day, Miss Belton's young musicians busked outside the supermarket, and collected enough money to buy a new clarinet.

Taking the plunge for the first time, Miss Dalton led her class to the Swimming Baths where she had them sampling the water for impurities and measuring its specific gravity. Also out for the first time was Mr. Vincent with his Art class, casing the neighbourhood for expanses of bare wall, fences and pavement on which to paint murals; open space on which to set sculptures; and public buildings on which to paste posters. Weaving through all their companions, panting past pedestrians, racing round motorists, and cheered on by their instructor, twenty-five athletic juveniles, ran ten times round the town in a mini-marathon.

It was not long before members of the public suspected something was going on which they ought to know about. The presence of a keen young photographer, with a distinct American accent, suggested to some that a film was being made and to others that an advertising stunt was being staged; a letter to the editor of the local give-away complained of a misuse of the public highway by groups of uniformed youngsters; and a telephone caller told the headmaster she had observed a number of his pupils 'obviously playing truant in the town centre'.

Fred C. Gee

The editor of the *Daily Pictorial* was not convinced that his readers would be interested in a group of kids cavorting about a church courtyard, or running wildly through the shops, but he did admit he might print the picture of a red-headed school girl talking to a bald-headed pensioner if Chuck could get a good story to go with it.

Rumours had reached the Chief Education Officer that Reginald Chalker's staff were on the rampage and there was speculation that one of the teachers was organising a campaign of resistance for party political reasons. No-one at the Education Office was quite sure which party the teacher supported but they had no doubt about who to suspect, or the party she opposed. News of these suspicions was leaked to all the local candidates, but none felt it important enough to bother about.

Apart from issuing words of encouragement at morning assemblies, Reginald Chalker kept a low profile and avoided interviews with the press or politicians. He did, however, inform his Education Office that the level of truancy at the school had fallen to zero. Morale among the teachers noticeably improved. Ideas for more and better out-of-school excursions came in from every department and the headmaster had to exercise diplomacy in determining which to support and which to discourage. However, when he became aware of the indifference being shown by party activists his attitude hardened and he endorsed any idea he considered likely to cause disruption and arouse attention. Before long the trickle of children appearing in the town during school hours became a flood, and no shopper or office worker could fail to observe the display of yellow socks and blue blazers flowing in all directions.

The sight of children pushing wheelbarrows and dogcarts was usually associated with the build-up to Bonfire Night; rarely, if ever, to gardening or commercial enterprises. A procession of that nature, with banners inviting donations of books, banknotes and sporting equipment, was now to be seen heading towards the town centre. Led by Miss Wordsworth, dressed shabbily for the occasion, and followed at the rear by Mr. Roper in a T-shirt, the column moved slowly through the streets, causing chaos on a scale unrivalled by election rallies.

In the residential neighbourhood, members of the third and fourth year history class were knocking on doors asking for any old photographs from family albums to add to the school's collection of local memorabilia. From the tone of their reception Mr. Godwin suspected the bright blue blazers and yellow socks they were wearing were misleading people into thinking they were canvassing for one of the contesting political parties. He therefore donned his academic gown and stood at the gates until doors were opened. No-one, he felt would mistake his apparel for that of a politician!

The fifth and sixth year historians were digging patches on the recreation ground looking for artefacts of archaeological interest. The oldest relic they unearthed was a tin of Balkan Sobranie tobacco, fortunately empty, which had probably been discarded by a spectator long before any of them were born.

Less concerned with Larkwood's past than its present or future, the fifth form of Miss Dalton's chemistry class were looking for water closets in which to take samples of the local water supply. The sixth form were dipping their buckets into the boating lake and the fountain in front of the church.

Still deputising for Sara Bishop in the French department, Miss Holland took her class of budding linguists into the showroom of a radio dealer where they tuned the sets on display to foreign stations and stored the programmes on pocket-sized tape recorders. Unknown to Frances, Miss Belton's music class had made a request to the local radio station for a record to be played by a favourite D.J. and it was being broadcast while Frances was in the shop. As a result there was so such excitement and noise that the recordings of all other programmes being made at the time became unintelligible.

With help from the Chemistry and Physics departments, Miss Snowdon offered her geographers a respite from mapping and supplied them with hydrogen filled balloons which they took to the town centre and released from outside the town hall. Buglers from Miss Belton's orchestra provided a fanfare, and each balloon carried a card to be read by whoever eventually picked it up, inscribed : ANOTHER DROP-OUT FROM OUR UNDERFUNDED SCHOOLS.

The Chief Education Officer was standing by his office window when the balloons went up. The expression could also be applied to the moment when he found one had fallen in his front garden and he read what it said on the cards. Aware of rumours about certain goings-on at the *Larkwood School*, he telephoned Reginald Chalker and demanded to know if he was aware of 'this outrage'. Mr. Chalker admitted that he did but said it was better to let the balloons take up the hot air being generated by staff feelings than to have them explode in the classroom - or worse, in a strike.

"That's all very well, but I'll have to answer to the Leader of the Council who will say this is an affront to his party at election time."

"Only if he feels that the cap fits, so to speak!"

"It'll be your cap, Chalker, which falls off if he does!"

Cards from fallen balloons were handed in or posted to party headquarters by people who either wanted to score a point or showed their indignation, according to their political allegiance. Thinking the publicity might influence the way votes would be cast, each party declared support for teachers, and wrote into its manifesto the importance of education.

None of the balloons got as far as Trimstead, but Bertrand was kept in the picture by frequent telephone calls from Reginald Chalker and in print by Chuck's contributions to the *Daily Pictorial*. There was a photograph of Miss Wordsmith pushing a barrow, headlined ENGLISH MISTRESS TAKES TO THE STREET, and underneath the picture was a caption saying: *Penniless Teacher Begs for Books*. On another page an editorial called for more investment in education, saying this would be essential if the country was to compete with its commercial rivals in the future. It concluded by asking if we really wanted our teachers to push carts around the streets begging for a living.

Weeks went by and the campaigns continued. Voting took place, and successful candidates were elected. Life in the local community continued as before. Shoppers prepared for Christmas and *Larkwood* students started rehearsing for the School Pantomime.

Bertrand reflected upon what had happened since he accepted the challenge to help the headmaster prevent a work-to-rule by his teachers. Unlike a pantomime, there had been no happy ending: the school was still underfunded, the teachers still underpaid, and the local politicians were still under the impression they were doing what their voters wanted. On the other hand, the public of Larkwood was better informed about its children's education, and morale at the school had been restored; fears of a strike had receded and relations with the local authority were mutually more respectful. It had not been one of Bertrand's most successful enterprises, but it had brought a sense of fun where gloom had been pervasive.

CHAPTER 17

It was Chuck's second Christmas with Vicky's family at Trimstead and he was now familiar with the Woodfellow rituals. Holly, mistletoe and a six-foot yew tree were gathered from the local plantation in the presence of the owner who went to school with Bertrand. An eighteen pound bird was selected from the flock of turkeys reared on a neighbouring farm. (Chuck associated turkey with Thanksgiving Day but was ready to eat it at any time.) On Christmas Eve a chest full of paper chains and coloured fairy lights was retrieved from the attic and the contents distributed about the house. Presents were parcelled up and placed at the foot of the tree for opening after breakfast on Christmas morning.

Brooches. silk squares and toilet goods were addressed to the ladies and socks, ties and leather wallets to the men, but interest was keenest in what had been bought for Bertrand. Jane's gift to her father-in-law was a large woollen rug which she imagined he might be glad to wrap round his legs when seated in a rocking chair in front of a log fire on a cold winter evening. Arthur, on the other hand, had given his father a walking stick with a horse's-head handle to encourage him to go out and exercise more often. Vicky gave him a hard-back copy of Cinderella, signed by each member of the cast in the *Larkwood School* pantomime, and Chuck gave a framed account of Bertrand's first exploit at the *Bigstall and Longstop Building Society* from a back number of *The Daily Pictorial.*

Vicky saved one present for Chuck until after the others had been opened. She took him to one side and whispered in his ear that she had something rather special to give him but said it was so well wrapped up that he might not be able to see it for a month or two. Chuck followed her eyes as she cast them towards the floor, and noticed they stopped short at her abdomen.

"Good gracious! You don't mean ...?"

"How did you guess?"

"Does your mother know?"

"Not yet. I thought you'd better be the first to know."

"Too darned right!"

"When shall I tell her?"

Chuck was about to answer when the telephone rang and they heard the Carters calling from America. This was not expected until later in the day because the previous year they were having lunch when the Carters called and the Christmas pudding had just arrived at table. As a result the ritual of pouring brandy over it and setting light to the rising vapour had to be abandoned. Anxious to prevent this happening a second time the Carters had risen early from their bed in Baltimore to make sure their greetings reached the Woodfellows well before it was lunch time in Trimstead.

With his father-in-law about to exchange views on the current economic situation, and his mother-in-law waiting to hear what the Carters were preparing for their lunch, Chuck grabbed the telephone and announced that he was going to have a baby. There followed a burst of laughter in all directions, before he corrected himself to say that Vicky was going to have the baby. Commotion ensued and only a calm reminder from Bertrand saved them from having cold turkey on Christmas Day as well as Boxing Day.

News of Vicky's pregnancy dominated conversation for the rest of the day on both sides of the Atlantic. The Carters debated whether they should go to England immediately, or wait for the christening; while Jane and Arthur agonised over whether Vicky should have the baby at home or in hospital.

When it seemed to Chuck that all options had been fully explored, he changed the subject by announcing that he had another surprise for Bertrand.

"Go on! You aren't a-goin' to tell us *you*'ve been hidin' somethin' up *your* jersey?"

Vicky blushed.

"Up my sleeve!" said Chuck. "Only this one won't take nine months to materialise. I've been asked to take you with me to meet the guys I work with."

Mr. Reid, editor of the *Daily Pictorial*, had known nothing of Bertrand Woodfellow until Chuck mentioned him at their office party shortly before Christmas. It had been a typically bibulous occasion and Chuck was being teased about his propensity for spotting the funny side of industrial disputes. His explanation that he was married to a woman whose grandfather specialised in settling strikes before they happened caused as much hilarity as if he had told a story about a one-legged pensioner climbing Everest on a three-legged donkey. Mr. Reid had enjoyed the joke, which he said suggested spirit from the bottle might have added something to Chuck's explanation, but then added: "I propose that Mr. Carter be asked to introduce us to his matrimonially acquired grandfather. You never know", he said, "one day *we* may be in need of his services."

Bertrand's visit to the *Daily Pictorial* early in the New Year coincided with a news item that the proprietor of the paper had taken a party of unemployed journalists to the Bahamas on his yacht and distributed them among the islands in small boats with a promise to pick them up and publish their survival stories if they were still there when he went back for them.

Spokesmen for the various chapels that are the trade unions of the printing industry took exception to the story and claimed that it cast a slur upon the integrity of their unemployed colleagues. Shortly before Bertrand's arrival they had met with the editor and threatened to walk out if the story was published or shown to be true. Mr. Reid was, therefore, delighted to be reminded of Bertrand's reputation for dealing with industrial disputes and greeted him with an invitation to tackle the one he was now faced with.

Bertrand was not aware that the crisis had only just arisen and suspected he had been lured to the premises under false pretences. Not wishing to commit himself, he looked quizzically at Chuck and asked the obvious question.

"I take it you've checked with your proprietor that the story is true?"

Mr. Reid looked uncomfortable.

Which made Chuck think Bertrand ought to have taken that for granted, but the editor was uncomfortable because he realised *he* had taken something for granted. The story had not been checked,

Chuck was quickly asked to show Bertrand round the building and bring him back to look at the evidence later. "Come back about twelve o'clock," said Mr. Reid, "and I'll take you both to lunch."

As soon as he was alone he called his secretary and dictated a cable to be sent immediately to the Chairman's yacht. It produced a prompt reply which reached the editor's desk as Chuck and Bertrand were returning from their tour. They were shown the cable without comment.

STORY SCANDALOUS STOP WILL SUE ANYONE WHO PUBLISHES IT STOP THAT INCLUDES YOU STOP.

Bertrand fixed the editor's gaze. "Would you say that was a denial or an admission?"

"The question is, will it satisfy the Chapels?"

They went to lunch and while they were gone copies of the cable were sent to Fathers of the various Chapels.

A deputation awaited the editor when he got back to his office. Instead of being relieved to know the story would not be published the men were furious at what they saw as an attempt to suppress it. They now believed it to be true.

Bertrand had been listening to the editor's views on a variety of subjects over lunch and had formed the opinion that he was not unsympathetic to the men who work for the *Daily Pictorial* and that his loyalty to the owner of the paper had not caused him to betray the work force that kept them all in business.

Initially, when the men had objected to the Chairman's extravagances in the Bahamas, Charles Reid felt it was none of their business and as long as they got a decent wage they ought to get on with their work. At that stage he envisaged Bertrand helping him subdue their reaction to the story but now the Chairman was making threats Charles felt he must ask Bertrand to help him uphold the freedom of the press.

"Do I publish and be damned? Or do I just say damn and forget it?"

"Would that be the end of it, do you think? There must be several people who have heard the story and know about your enquiry. Can you keep all of them quiet?"

"I'm not the one who wants to keep them quiet! I'm just supposed to make sure everyone knows the old man will sue them if they repeat the story."

"Won't that make matters worse? Unless you know exactly who has heard the story and who they may have passed it on to, you'll be telling people who haven't heard it, and whetting their curiosity. I'd say you were on a hiding to nothing!"

"Apart from the staff, I'll have to tell my opposite numbers about his threat to sue."

"Won't that give them a better story?"

"It happens so often, it won't even be news!"

Bertrand was bewildered. If there was no story, then what were they worried about? On the other hand, if the original report was true, then surely there was a story.

Charles began to think aloud. "I daresay we can keep it in-house because the men here don't want to admit it might be true, which is why the Chapels wanted me to kill the story in the first place. The problem now is how can I stop them cooking up an excuse to go on strike just to spite the old devil!"

"I take it you don't care much for your Chairman?"

"Oh, but I do. I *care* for him all the time. That's my job. He pays my salary, but I wish he'd pay a bit more attention to the feelings of those who make his millions for him!"

"Do you really think there'll be a strike?"

"Yes. I'm sure of it. ... Unless you can perform one of your miracles."

Bertrand pondered. He was not quite sure which side the editor was on.

"If they *were* to strike, where would your sympathies lie: with the men or the Chairman?"

"With the paper. That's bigger than both!"

"Right, but could you stand up to the Chairman - in the interests of the paper?"

"Is that hypothetical, or have you something in mind?"

Bertrand was not ready to reveal what was forming in his mind so he asked another question. "Could you rely on the staff to stick with you if you did take on the Chairman?"

Charles Reid was suddenly alarmed. He had often criticised the Chairman, but never to his face. No-one had ever done that and survived.

"I'll tell you what I would do if I were in your position," said Bertrand. "But, of course, it might mean I wouldn't be in your position for very long."

By the time Bertrand left the building pages were being put together for the following day's edition. He returned to Trimstead with an assurance from the editor that his suggestions would be carefully considered but it sounded very much like the customary response to unwanted contributors, and Bertrand did not expect to hear anything further. Except, possibly, a groan from Chuck!

In fact, Chuck had very little to say to Bernard when Vicky telephoned at the week-end. This made Bertrand think Chuck had been offended by being left out of the afternoon session with his editor. Or, perhaps, the editor had blamed him for wasting his time with unsuitable ideas. All that Chuck would say in reply to Bertrand's questions was that he would probably be hearing from Mr. Reid in the next day or two.

A copy of Monday's *Daily Pictorial* arrived by post on Tuesday morning, addressed to Mr. Woodfellow Senior.

Bertrand saw at once that something was missing. In fact, the front page of the paper, which usually included a large photograph, headlined or captioned, was entirely blank. When a copy of Tuesday's edition arrived on Wednesday morning it confirmed that Charles Reid had adopted one of his suggestions for there was again a large open space on the front page, except for the silhouette of a yacht in the top left hand corner. There was still no wording on the page.

Bernard decided he could not wait until Thursday for the next instalment so, after breakfast, he set off for the metropolis to get a copy of the current edition while it was still on the bookstalls. Normally there would have been a plentiful supply of all the daily newspapers on sale at the station, but he found the *Daily Pictorials* had been sold out by the time he got there. Thwarted, though inwardly excited, he made straight for the *Pictorial's* offices where he took a copy from the counter and sat down to read it. To his delight the front page picture spot now showed a wide stretch of beach in the bottom right hand sector with the silhouette of a yacht still where it was the day before.

He was debating whether to ask if the editor would see him when Chuck walked out of the lift, heading for the street. Bertrand promptly intercepted him, waving the paper with a feigned expression of annoyance.

"Did you know about this when I spoke to you on Sunday," he boomed, "and was it you who's been sending me copies through the post ev'ry day?"

Chuck saw a familiar gleam in Bertrand's eyes. "Did we forgot to pay the postage!"

"Who forgot to fill the front page?"

"Who forgot to tell me what you and Charlie Reid were up to that afternoon when I left you in his office?"

Bertrand took him by the arm. "Ssh! Walls have ears, as we used to say! Sit down and tell me how much you know."

Chuck dropped the pretence and congratulated his old partner. "You've done it again, haven't you! The old man's delighted: says you're a genius. We've got every other paper in the country fishing for what it's all about. Sales are up, and letters are pouring in from readers asking if it's a competition."

Bertrand looked worried. "Any news yet from the Chairman?"

Chuck followed his thinking. "Daresay he went out of contact after sending that cable. Unless, of course, he's entertaining his lawyers."

"I hope Mr. Reid has a good lawyer!"

"He's got the Chapel supporting him. That ought to help."

Bertrand accepted an invitation to stay with Chuck and Vicky for the rest of the week so he could be around when the sequels were published.

Palm trees were added to the scene in Thursday's edition, and on Friday there was the outline of a dinghy between the yacht and the beach. But, still no captions or explanations.

On Saturday, the dinghy was on the shoreline and men were shown running across the beach towards the palm trees.

Fred C. Gee

CHAPTER 18

Lord Shillingsworth began his career as a newspaper owner when he published an undercover magazine in the sixth form at High School. For photocopies of this, typed on his mother's portable Remington, he charged a shilling, which earned him tuppence profit. That, of course, was before English currency went metric and when inflation was a word associated almost exclusively with the blowing up of balloons.

Progressing rapidly from this primitive, and occasionally pornographic, publishing venture, Jimmy Penrose found a lucrative livelihood in the second-hand book market, buying copies of paper-backs and periodicals at twenty-five percent of their cover price and selling them at fifty percent. A family holiday in Denmark introduced him to a new source of exciting material in glossy covers with nude pictures and tales of sex. Jimmy's clientele broadened and his profits soared.

By the time he was thirty, Mr. Penrose had a respectable business, with an office in Soho, trading in posters and all forms of freely available publicity produced by the film industry. Collectors were not only the elderly and middle-aged indulging in nostalgia but also their children and grandchildren venerating the screen stars of yesterday. Profit on sales was now 100 percent and Jimmy was getting rich.

At forty, he introduced the public to Penrose Publications, an enterprise exclusively concerned with the printing of books and journals about films and anyone involved in the writing or making of films. Then, as the spread of television took the small screen into people's homes, TV was added to the business and Penrose products appeared on shelves in retail shops and railway stations. Jimmy was now a wealthy businessman, experienced in company affairs, and a shrewd supporter of the political party then in power. It was no surprise, when that party was looking for candidates to uphold their representation in the Upper House, that Jimmy Penrose was offered a peerage and took the title Lord Shillingsworth of Soho.

His purchase of *The Daily Pictorial* was controversial at the time, for there were many who feared the paper would adopt the style and format of a Penrose glossy, but this did not happen. Aware that others had raised their circulation (and that of their readers) with photographs of teenage breasts on page three and elsewhere, the *Pictorial* opted for a policy of no nudes. When readers continued to defect to the rival tabloids he introduced a feature called Exotic Art in which cultural depictions of sexual attraction from ancient and oriental sources, long out of copyright and inexpensive to reproduce, were serialised on the centre pages and proved highly successful. The *Daily Pictorial* regained its readership, and Lord Shillingsworth was spared to spend another holiday away from the boardroom, on board his yacht.

Puzzled by the source of the story about his entertaining and marooning unemployed journalists, Lord Jimmy, as he liked to be called by those to whom he offered hospitality, took refuge in the combination of blond and bottle and tried to forget the incident. Confident that his threat of litigation would stop any spread of the story, he made no attempt to hurry home or to resume communication with his office. Charles Reid was allowed a clear week in which to divert his readers and amuse his staff. Rival editors were left guessing the significance of what seemed a suicidal lapse of judgement, and media pundits vied with each other to evaluate the public's reaction to an unconventional use of the front page. Newsagents throughout the country clamoured for back numbers as the debate continued and advertising agents saw a new approach by which to gain readership attention.

Lord Jimmy became Lord Shillingsworth again as soon as he was back in England. On returning from America he was met at the airport by a posse of newsmen anxious to ask him what he knew about the front page pictures that had aroused so much interest in his newspaper while he was away.

"Nothing," he replied. "I've been on holiday."

Without knowing how near the nub she had struck, one of the reporters asked if the yacht in the pictures was the one on which he had been cruising.

"You'd better ask the editor," he told her, "I haven't seen the pictures and I don't remember being photographed."

His arrival at the offices of the *Daily Pictorial* was anticipated with apprehension by the staff, from the doorkeeper inwards. They had been told the editor's struggle with the Chairman was in defence of the freedom of the press, but the scent of scandal was still in their nostrils as many of them knew the story and the attempt to suppress it.

The front page picture that morning repeated the scene developed during the previous week: a desert island with men scrambling across the beach from a dinghy on the shoreline. This time, however, there was no sign of the yacht from which they had come. A copy of the paper was on his desk when the Chairman returned and by the time he had studied it, together with the other six issues, he was in no doubt that they depicted the story he had tried to suppress. "Tell the editor I want him in my office *immediately*," he bellowed to his secretary.

Charles Reid had no illusions about what would follow. He entered the Chairman's room with the confidence of a schoolboy who had been caught writing rude words about the teacher on a blackboard.

"What the devil is the meaning of all this?" he was asked.

"I can't answer that without breaching your injunction."

Lord Shillingsworth exploded.

"How dare you! I'll see you through the courts for this."

"Won't that break the story you wanted to suppress?"

"I'll break you, Mr. Reid. You're fired! Right now! Get out!"

News of the editor's dismissal was quickly round the building and staff in all departments approached their chapels ready to stop work. They were told there was a long-term plan to get the editor reinstated, and that in the meantime they should carry on working. The plan, they were told, would become clear before long.

Lord Shillingsworth sent for the Deputy Editor.

Sandy MacQuill was a less florid personality than Charlie Reid but he displayed a brief flush of nervousness as he set off for the Chairman's office. He carried the benediction of the editorial staff to encourage him, but there were no niceties of greeting or introduction as he was shown in.

"How much do you know about what has been going on while I was away?"

"Very little, m'Lord."

"You've seen the pictures, though?"

"Och, yes, but we're all guessin' what they're about!"

"What is your guess, then?"

"I think they're meant to arouse curiosity and raise the circulation. What you might call ... a cunning come-on!"

The Chairman stared at Sandy, unsure whether to believe in his honesty, or was it naivety? In the end he decided to give him the benefit of doubt.

"I've just suspended your editor; could *you* carry on?"

Sandy had been briefed for this, and urged to accept.

"If that is your Lordship's wish, I'll do m' best."

The newly appointed editor returned to his room where colleagues from Features, Film and Drama, Radio and Television, Sports, Travel, Foreign Affairs, Fashion, Finance and the Weekly Supplement had gathered to hear the outcome of his meeting. He wondered if they had come to support him or commiserate with Mr. Reid.

Charles Reid himself had left Sandy in no doubt on that score. They were all there to support him - so long as he pursued the policy of standing firm against the Chairman's interference with editorial prerogative.

"You don't reckon I'll be in th' job fer long, then?" said Sandy, with undisguised foreboding.

They were still laughing when the telephone rang.

"It's for you, Charlie."

"If it's the editor they want, it's for you now, old man."

"No, it's someone called Bertie. Says he's returning your call."

Mr. Reid had telephoned Trimstead to tell Bertrand of his fate, only to be told he was staying with Chuck and Vicky. The message had been passed on, and Bertrand had lost no time in phoning back. He was not surprised by the news but concerned at what would happen to Mr. Reid. Charles told him he was being looked after by the chapel and said his deputy had agreed to carry on where he left off. Bertrand assured him he would continue to collaborate with his successor.

No mention was made in the paper next day of the change of editor but readers were surprised to find the same picture on the front page as was there the previous day. This time, however, there was a caption. It said:

... *Two hundred years ago, to-day, Fletcher Christian and the Bounty mutineers landed on Pitcain Island.* ...

Some readers checked the story in encyclopaedias and found it was true, others thought it was part of the joke. Cynics said it must be a trick to win more readers. Lord Shillingsworth was delighted and full of praise for his new editor. But Sandy knew he had the mysterious Bertie to thank for an alibi which enabled him to bring the allegory to a close at the right moment.

Reaction among the other dailies varied from relief that the game was now over to suspicion that an underlying truth had been omitted. By lunch time news had leaked to the local bars that Charlie Reid was no longer editing the *Daily Pictorial*, and a columnist of the evening paper suggested he had fallen foul of an unpopular Chairman.

Lord Shillingsworth was shown the offending column before he left for an evening at the theatre and sent angrily for Sandy MacQuill.

"Find out who's been blabbing, and make sure you kill the innuendo!"

"Would you, m'lord, have any suggestion to offer of how...?"

"You're the editor; that's for you to decide!"

MacQuill wondered if this was the editorial freedom he was fighting for.

A call to stop the presses was usually reserved for when some exceptional news came in after the first editions had started printing. Sandy could not remember when this last happened but he had no qualms about asking for such action on this occasion. Staff from all departments were alerted and pages were recast, while Sandy prepared a new editorial to meet the Chairman's command.

Next morning the readers could hardly believe their eyes. The *Daily Pictorial* had been printed in double spacing! Every story on every page had been trimmed to half its original length, except the editorial which was printed in bold capital letters. The gist of the editorial was that unfounded rumours had identified the front page commemorative with a contemporary event and were seeking to implicate a highly respectable member of the media in a scandalous fiction. The editor's punch line read as follows:-

The present edition of the paper is designed to show there is nothing to be read between the lines.

MacQuill's dismissal came as no surprise to anyone. His chapel protested to the Chairman and demanded his reinstatement, with that of Mr. Reid, but Lord Shillingsworth claimed they had brought the paper into disrepute and must pay the price. Members of staff renewed their call for an all out strike, but Mr. Reid urged them to keep up the campaign he started, saying it would have more effect than to withdraw their labour. To reinforce his message, he gave them an outline of what might still be in store for the Chairman and reluctantly they accepted his advice.

Meanwhile the Chairman secured the services of a replacement editor from a nearby provincial newspaper. Unaware of the circumstances of his appointment, Mr.

Jonathan Blount arrived to find no enthusiasm for his presence and little willingness to co-operate with him. After a cheerless initiation he was even more depressed to discover the edition brought to him that evening from the printers differed substantially from the one he had set for printing. At first sight everything on the front page looked fine. A photograph of Lord Shillingsworth at the opera had pride of place and there was a headline proclaiming the circulation of the paper had increased by ten percent in the past month. When Mr Blount turned to the inside pages, however, he was horrified to see that all the advertisements, on which the prosperity of the paper depended, had been printed upside-down. When the Chairman received his copy he looked no further than the front page, which pleased him because it showed him supporting the arts, and he assumed the rebellion had ended.

Next morning there were calls to the office from several advertising agencies congratulating the paper on helping them sell their clients' products.

Heartened by this, Mr. Blount remembered the well known showbiz maxim 'more of the same is the name of the game' and planned to repeat the inversion of advertisements in the next issue, but his satisfaction was short lived. The presses were already running when he discovered the printers had re-aligned the advertisements and inverted the text of his editorial. By a stroke of luck, the Chairman was absent in Edinburgh and so missed the excitement caused by this latest act of resistance.

Attempts by the new editor to avoid a third fiasco failed miserably. He insisted that in future everything should be set in the upright position, even if it disappointed the handful of supporters, but he underestimated the printers. They printed a number of advertisements correctly aligned but above each was a head-line intended for future articles. On the Sports Page an advertisement for dog food appeared beneath the headline BOXER IN COMA, and on the Money Page a headline CRASH ON TOKYO EXCHANGE appeared above an advertisement for Japanese motorcars. The Music Page had a headline saying SINGER LOSES VOICE, which was underscored by an advertisement for a security firm, and the Gardening section carried an advertisement for slimming pills beneath the heading WEEDS ARE UNWELCOME.

Realising he now had no hope of controlling matters Mr. Blount wept into his spectacles and spared the Chairman a further dismissal by tendering his resignation.

At this juncture, Lord Shillingsworth decided it was time to become Jim Penrose again. Confident his background in journalism would serve him through the crisis, he announced that until further notice he would edit the paper himself. There was consternation in the chapels but determination among the printers. Despite strict supervision and threats of instant dismissal for any perversity, the *Daily Pictorial* appeared on the streets next morning printed entirely in red.

Normally when the Chairman of a company saw red it was time for all levels of staff to take cover. When that optical euphemism became a physical reality, and was shared with the public at large, there was nowhere for anyone to hide. Not even his secretary dared to disturb Lord Shillingsworth, and many employees opted for their annual leave.

For Lord Shillingsworth there was no escape. Not even the occasional reversion to Jim Penrose could release him from his current dilemma. As Jim Penrose he would probably have fired the entire staff and recruited afresh, or put the whole business up for sale and moved on to a new enterprise. As Lord Shillingsworth of Soho, he told himself, he must show statesmanship, and leadership, and ... if necessary, brinkmanship. Whatever the ship, at all costs he had to weather the storm.

His inclination was to tighten the controls; to take more authority into his own hands and to cast off all encumbrances. His reputation was to shout, to blame others and to bully his way out of trouble. Yet he knew from experience that having authority was no guarantee of getting obedience. Even to have the power to give orders was not enough unless you also had the means to carry them out.

Jim Penrose had learned one rule that had stood him in good stead all his life. Whenever he failed to push an obstacle over he worked his way round it. But, now he was at the top the only way he could go round was to go down a step and that meant going back. Pride then became the obstacle.

It was pride that was blocking his view now. In spite of suspending two of his senior editors for what seemed to be a dereliction of duties, and despite the introduction of an outsider with apparently no accomplices, production of the paper remained out of control. Yet, his advisers told him, circulation was increasing.

He was struggling to reconcile these facts when the telephone rang.

"I thought I said no calls, Miss Dainty."

"Yes, sir, but this is special. I've just heard that we've been voted Newspaper of the Year."

"Who by? The Daily Sludge?"

"No. The Guild of Editors and Correspondents."

"What do they know about it!"

Before he could say more, Miss Dainty added that the Advertising Manager had been plagued all morning by agencies demanding more space for their clients in the *Daily Pictorial.*

"To complain, I suppose!"

"To take advertisements, I'm told."

Another call came in. It was from a television company inviting Lord Shillingsworth to join a Panel that evening for a topical discussion on media matters. Miss Dainty asked the caller to hold while she consulted his diary but, in fact, consulted Lord Shillingsworth. He brightened for a moment and accepted; then realised he would not know how to explain the apparent change of policy which had brought sudden notoriety to his paper.

"You'd better find Charlie Reid and ask him to come and see me. Tell him to come *at once!*"

"That may be difficult," said Miss Dainty, calmly. "I understand Mr. Reid and Mr. MacQuill are looking for new employment."

"Well you'd better hurry then, before they do anything so foolish!"

Miss Dainty knew quite well where to find Mr. Reid, who had never strayed far from his old department. Her loyalty to the Chairman had not prevented her from remaining on friendly terms with an old colleague. She gave him just enough background to explain the reason for his summons.

"Come in, Charles, and sit down; I'd like to talk to you."

"What about? I thought I'd been fired."

Lord Shillingsworth uncharacteristically fidgeted.

"Maybe there's been a little misunderstanding," he said. "Possibly on my part. Possibly on yours. ...Tell me, why did you decide to turn the *Daily Pictorial* into a national comic?"

"Is that what you think it is?"

"I understand it's now the Newspaper of the Year. ... According to the Guild of Editors. ...Is that significant?"

"Possibly!"

"I don't like being made a laughing stock."

"I didn't like being made a puppet!"

"Did you say puppet, or poppet?"

Charles could tell he was not trying to be funny.

"I said puppet."

Lord Shillingsworth was silent. Then he cleared his throat. "I think you'd better explain."

Charles accepted the invitation. "I sent a cable to your yacht asking for information and expected a denial, not an ultimatum. There was no trust that I would act in your best interest. Or that I would use my own discretion. You treated me, and then Sandy, like cabin boys, there to take your orders."

"Hold on! If it's trust you're talking about, why did you think there might be any truth in such a silly story? Shouldn't you have trusted me?"

"Why? You didn't deny it. You just said it was scandalous. That sounded like there *was* a story in it."

The noble Lord reflected, and was untypically contrite.

"Will you believe me if I deny it now?"

"Yes, if you say so."

"Well, I do deny it. There weren't any unemployed journalists on board that yacht. They were unsuccessful contenders in a beauty contest. If anyone started the rumour it was probably a disgruntled chaperone! Now do you see why I didn't want the story serialised?"

Charles Reid could now relax. "Did you put them ashore on the islands?"

"That's where they came from in the first place."

At last they could laugh. Lord Shillingsworth stood up and held out his hand. "Will you come back and edit the Newspaper of the Year?"

"Only if I have your assurance there will be no more proprietorial interference."

"Where the devil did you get that expression?"

"You're not dodging the question, are you?"

"Damn you, no! Come back and I'll see that no-one interferes with you again. I'll even give you a seat on the Board so *you* can do the interfering!"

"What about Sandy MacQuill?"

"When you're on the Board you can have him back if you think he deserves it."

"And Mr. Blount - what about him?"

"Ah, well! We could offer him to an advertising agency. Unless you think that would be interfering?"

CHAPTER 19

The return of Charles Reid and Sandy MacQuill to their previous editorial duties was greeted by their colleagues with relief and seen as evidence of victory over their proprietor. Lord Shillingsworth shared the relief but denied defeat. He considered he had acted magnanimously by reinstating two recalcitrants.

In Trimstead, Chuck was enjoying a quiet drink with Vicky and Bertrand. He raised his glass 'to Old Bertie'.

"Why me?" said Bertrand, feigning innocence.

"Because, once more, you have shown us the power of wit over weapons."

"Hey, steady on! Are you sure it wasn't wit over wisdom?"

Chuck looked bemused.

Bertrand confessed doubts about his involvement in the newspaper affair. He set out, he said, to see how a newspaper was put together and found himself watching it being torn apart. "When your editor asked me for my advice I thought it was to avoid a strike by people who wanted to show solidarity with fellow journalists they thought were being ill-treated by your proprietor. It seems that I ended up helping the editor strike at the proprietor."

"You helped him get his job back," said Chuck.

"Yes, but once it became a family feud I should have got out!"

"It was more than that, you know," said Chuck, being untypically serious. "It was a matter of principle: whether the editor should have the last word in running the paper, or the owner."

"If you had been the owner, wouldn't you have said you were entitled to run it?"

"Maybe, but if I were the editor I'd claim I had a responsibility to the readers."

"Interesting you should say that! I was wondering where they came in. Aren't they as likely to be misled by an editor as a wealthy proprietor?"

Vicky, who had listened to the dialogue with growing impatience, decided it was time to intervene.

"Speaking as a mere reader, I'd say it was better to have an editor who can be replaced if he oversteps the mark than a tycoon who has no-one to kick him out if he goes wrong."

Bertrand was too fond of his granddaughter to contradict her, but he pointed out gently there may be little to choose between the two. Editors and owners, he said, need to sell copies - and neither will be too scrupulous about the means. "How many readers, do you think, bother to check if they are being told the truth?" Most people, he suggested, choose the paper they think will tell them what they want to be told.

"Grandpa, you're an old cynic!"

"He's right, Vicky," said Chuck, "but I guess our readers know a good paper when they see one."

The problem for Charles Reid now that he had his job back was that many of his readers had come to expect the unexpected. Could he, he wondered, keep those readers if he reverted to the old-style *Daily Pictorial?* Conversely, could he keep up a regular flow of surprises when there was no longer the impetus for battle? He looked again at the list of ideas suggested by Bertrand in their campaign against the Chairman. One, in particular, appealed to him because it offered a means of keeping up the morale of staff which was now higher than ever before.

Heads of departments, leading columnists and correspondents, received an invitation to a Reception in the Editor's Office which they assumed to be a celebration party to mark Charlie Reid's return. Their assumption seemed to be confirmed when they were asked to participate in a game of 'General Post'.

Most of them were familiar with the parlour game, which they remembered playing in their youth, and they formed up on opposite sides of the room waiting for instructions to change places. What the editor had in mind, however, was more a gimmick than a game. To start with, he wanted the Theatre Correspondent to write about the proceedings in Parliament, the Political Editor to spend a week or more on Drama, the Industrial Correspondent to change duties with the Gardening expert, and the Financial Editor to take over the Weather slot. Sports writers were offered Music, Travel writers Domestic Affairs; and on he plodded through the staff list until all the assignments had been rearranged. Each one was greeted with a gasp of horror or disbelief but Mr. Reid was remorseless. Every month, he said, he wanted them to change places with someone else until all permutations had been exhausted.

"Not to mention the public!" was one retort.

"Or us!" was another. "How long do you think it will be before we're all exhausted?"

"I'm exhausted now," said a third.

The meeting was about to break up when Sandy MacQuill reminded them of the paper's reputation for enterprise and novelty. He said the Editor's idea was a challenge to their journalistic talents. They emptied their glasses and dispersed.

Charles Reid had paired himself with Sandy MacQuill and together they wrote an article about the man they held responsible for the paper's change of fortune. It appeared a few days later under a banner headline:

WHITE KNIGHT OR BLACKLEG?

The article told of a man in his mid-sixties who had retired from the noise and bustle of business but was devoting his skills and experience to imaginative ways of dealing with industrial disputes.

It began: *From an early age he found favour with his friends by having fun with them. When faced with the need to fight he used fun instead of fists. Failing to see the funny side, his victims often fled. Few suffered more than damage to their pride.*

And continued: *As a young man, he grew up in a village where wealth and opportunities were in short supply. Craftsmanship was on the wane, but he taught himself to be a carpenter. When tourists arrived on the scene and bought furniture for the antique trade, he set up in business to make replicas. It amused him to think there would always be something for the villagers to offer when genuine supplies ran out. His small workshop became a large factory, and the impecunious young man became a wealthy manufacturer. When he retired he passed the business to his son and, but for a chance remark, he might have spent the rest of his life in quiet seclusion. But that was not to be. Those who work hard at their jobs often find it hard to relax when their working days are over. The carpenter, who had never wasted a nail or thrown away an off-cut from his stock of timber, regretted his retirement and longed for a new outlet to engage his energy. The opportunity came when a friend of the family happened to say he was looking for a way of persuading his staff not to take to the picket lines. The challenge was irresistible. If he could stop fights with a little bit of fun why not a strike? So began a new career in which he used comedy and mockery to expose cases of stubbornness, unfairness and exploitation. Employees have got better terms from their employers, and employers better understanding from their staff, without strikes or lock-outs, damaging publicity or loss of earnings.*

After digressing into the economics of industrial unrest, the authors concluded:-

The Daily Pictorial has reason to be grateful to this judicious jester for ideas that have improved its management structure, enlivened its pages, and increased its circulation.

Following the publication of this article, the paper was inundated with enquiries to know more about the person to whom it referred. Charles Reid was delighted, and fanned the flames of curiosity by refusing to give any further information.

Bertrand was sent a copy of the article by post with the editor's compliments. Amused and flattered, he telephoned the editor to thank him and to appeal for anonymity. Mr. Reid told him people were asking to be put in touch with him and, reluctantly, Bertrand agreed to call some of them back.

He returned the call of one company executive in dispute with a Trades Union, but the advice he offered led to him getting an abusive message from a Shop Steward telling him to go back to sticking glue on wood and to leave the workers to look after their own affairs.

The solution of industrial disputes was soon the subject of articles and correspondence in all the national newspapers. Some criticised the *Daily Pictorial* for trivialising a serious issue; others explicitly stated their preference for traditional methods of problem solving. As the debate intensified, Bertrand was invited to speak at seminars and to give lectures to professional and educational audiences.

One such invitation came from America where he was offered free transport and accommodation to address a congress of industrial experts and to appear afterwards on a televised discussion with Trade Union leaders. This he found hard to resist but his inexperience in public speaking led him to decline the offer. Instead, he arranged to send a fluent American speaker as his deputy. It was Chuck's reward for loyalty, and an opportunity for him to take Vicky to visit his parents.

Although shy of making speeches, Bertrand had not been slow to express his views on management and industrial relations to friends and members of his family, so they were not surprised when he consented to face the cameras in conversation with a well known broadcaster on a British television network. He saw it as an opportunity to commend his philosophy to the general public and prepared for it with undisguised enthusiasm.

What he was not prepared for when he entered the studio was the intensity of light and proximity of the cameras. Sweat had already begun to drip from his forehead while they were getting into position, and he soon understood why they called it a warming up procedure.

Eventually a red light appeared in front of him and the interview began.

"Good evening, Mr. Woodfellow, you seem to have acquired the reputation of being a kind of Mr. Fixit. How did that come about?"

"Well, I suppose I've always been a bit of a rebel. Didn't like to think anything was impossible. Always ready to try out a new idea. Even when people said it wouldn't work."

"Especially then?"

"Perhaps. That always made the challenge more fun."

"Ah, fun ... you use that word a lot, don't you? Has life always been fun for you?"

"Well, I weren't born wi' a silver spoon in m' mouth, but I were quite young when I learned how to get my own way with a smile..... or by making somebody laugh."

"Didn't they ever get cross with you for that?"

"Oh, ah, but that made it more fun, you see, cos by then I'd usually got what I wanted!"

"And have you gone on getting what you wanted all your life?"

"Oh no! I've changed my mind too often to be able to say that."

"You've changed your mind about what you want, but not the way of getting it?"

"It's been one way of getting it when others have failed. Let's say it's been less stress than struggle, and better for the blood pressure!"

"Yours, maybe, but what about your victims? I don't suppose they've always seen the funny side?"

"I don't often make fun of people - only situations."

"Do all situations have a funny side?"

"If you look for it, most of them do. The trouble is not everyone knows where to look."

"Would that be your secret then; knowing where to look?"

"I don't think of it as a secret: more a habit, you might say."

"Quite a habit! And like most habits, I suppose, hard to kick, even when you retire?"

"Harder still now I've time to look at other people's problems instead of my own."

"You make it sound like fun, but you take problem solving seriously, don't you?"

"Yes I do. Because I think our methods of solving problems are out of date. Take strikes, for example. They're the conventional outcome of industrial disputes, but they nearly always end up costing both sides more than they are worth. Think of the aggro. they cause to people who have nothing to do with what the dispute is about; and the unpleasantness and spitefulness that goes on long after the strike is over. I reckon it's worth looking for more civilised ways of settling that kind of dispute?"

"Aren't you a bit out-of-date yourself on that one? I thought strikes were becoming a thing of the past."

"Not yet, I'm afraid. Most Unions still see it as their chief weapon in the power game."

"You call it a game. Is that how *you* see it?"

"I think commerce is a game. For every one who wins another loses. Most games have an element of chance, but nearly all favour the strong. It's 'not done' to cheat, although some do, but there's nothing against using a little cunning to gain an advantage. That's what I try to do if I think the dice are loaded."

"Is that a more civilised way of solving a dispute?"

"It's more cost effective, less painful, and different. You see, that's all I'm trying to say. I may be a pig-headed countryman but I don't keep my head in the same trough and I don't pretend I've got the answer to all our problems. All I offer is an alternative. We live in a changing world and old methods are not untouchable. Artists and architects are always looking for new ways to express their skills. My hope is that one day we shall all find ways to resolve our differences without causing distress to so many others."

"And what you recommend is comedy instead of confrontation?"

"A sense of humour is a great de-fuser!"

The interviewer heard his producer telling him to bring the discussion to a close so he smiled at Bertrand and led him towards a finish.

"You seem to have been demonstrating that to a lot of people. Now, how would you advise *me* if I were to say I was having trouble with my employers?"

Bertrand was taken by surprise. This had not been mentioned in their rehearsal. Seeing a grin on his interviewer's face, however, he regarded it as an invitation to relax.

"I'd suggest you ask your viewers to write letters to the Chairman and Board of Directors, and forget to put stamps on!"

The interviewer laughed, but felt it wise to admit to the audience that he was only joking. Bertrand, however, was not going to let him off the hook.

"Let me put the question the other way round? Suppose your employer was in dispute with *you* and others on his staff. What advice do you think I should give *him*?"

"Oh dear! I can't imagine!"

"I think I would suggest he should arrange for animals and children to be present whenever you appear before the cameras."

"Good night, Mr. Woodfellow, and thank you."

Bertrand was very tired when he got back to Trimstead. There was a friendly greeting from all the family, who had been admiring his performance, but his one desire now was to go to sleep. Before he could do that he slumped into a comfortable chair and told his admirers he had made up his mind to stop meddling in other people's problems.

Vicky saw he was about to close his eyes and whispered gently: "Dear grandpa, the trouble is that other people won't stop having them."

An hour later when he woke, Vicky took him a glass of his favourite brandy. "Thank you, my dear," he said wearily. "You know, I've been dreaming. I'm not sure where it all began, but I seem to have set up in business with your husband as a consultant. We had a big staff and a large office and lots of clients. Then just as I woke up Chuck appeared and said the staff wanted more money and were coming out on strike!"

Chuck had been listening and asked Bertrand what he would have said had it *not* been a dream.

"P'raps I'd have said we must both have been dreamin' to let 'em think of doing such a thing!"

THE END

www.ingramcontent.com/pod-product-compliance
Lightning Source LLC
Chambersburg PA
CBHW071704090426
42738CB00009B/1657